# MY LODGE

SIMPLE WAS MY LODGE
OF BIRCH
PURE WAS THE WATER
THAT I DRANK
SWIFT WAS THE CANOE
THAT CARRIED ME
STRAIGHT WAS THE ARROW
THAT PROTECTED ME
WILD WAS THE MEAT
THAT FED ME
SWEET WAS THE
SUGAR MAPLE
STRONG WERE THE HERBS
THAT SUSTAINED ME
GREAT WAS MY MOTHER
THE EARTH

-DUKE REDBIRD

## DEDICATION

TO ALL THOSE WHO CONTINUE TO TEACH
THE OLD WAYS AND TRADITIONS OF NATIVE
CULTURE TO THE NEXT GENERATION

· AND TO ·

THE MILLIONS OF RESPONSIBLE HUNTERS ,
ANGLERS AND NATURALISTS WHO TREAT THE
EARTH WITH RESPECT ,  ENSURING OUR
CHILDREN WILL ENJOY THE BEAUTY OF NATURE
AND THE WILDERNESS AS WE HAVE

# NATIVE INDIAN
# WILD GAME ,
# FISH
# &
# WILD FOODS
# COOKBOOK

✳

## RECIPES FROM NORTH AMERICAN
## NATIVE COOKS

Edited by David Hunt

CASTLE BOOKS
Edison, New Jersey

# THE NATIVE INDIAN WILD GAME, FISH AND WILD FOODS COOKBOOK

Cover Design :        Brian S. Reese

Published by
CASTLE BOOKS
A Division of Book Sales, Inc.
114 Northfield Avenue
Edison, New Jersey 08837

© 1992 by Fox Chapel Publishing Co.

ISBN 0-7858-0707-1

Published by arrangement with and permission of
Fox Chapel Publishing Co.

MANUFACTURED IN THE UNITED STATES OF AMERICA.

# TABLE OF

# CONTENTS

# AND RECIPE INDEX

## ·CHAPTER SEVEN · ............................................188
### SAUCES, MARINADES, STUFFINGS, BATTERS AND BREADS....

## ·CHAPTER EIGHT · ............................................201
### EDIBLE WILD PLANTS , NUTS , BERRIES AND WILD BAKING ..
### WILD PLANTS - IDENTIFICATION AND INFORMATION

**I.**

# INTRODUCTION

*"Hunting is a holy occupation" - Navajo saying*

There is something uniquely meaningful in eating a meal of wild foods. The act of hunting, fishing and gathering is a powerful direct link reminding us of how we rely on the earth for our very existence.

This cookbook is a celebration of cookery from the wilds. It is fitting that all the recipes here come from Native Indian cooks, for this culture has always been inextricably connected with the land and a proper understanding of our relationships and responsibilities to nature.

Many of these recipes are traditional, dating back hundreds of years. Others are more recent using modern ingredients and spices. Every one is delicious.

We are indebted to Brenda Anstey, Beverly Brown and others of the Lovesick Lake Native Women's Association in Ontario, Canada. Many of these recipes came out of a two year project they conducted; researching and document-ing information, stories and recipes. They are women of vision and are currently working on raising funds for a camp/conference center dedicating to passing on Native culture and traditions.*

We would also like to thank the following groups for their information and encouragement.

Theresa Thorpe, American Indian Heritage Foundation

Leanne Pauley, American Indian Women's Service League

The Crazy Horse Memorial Foundation

Office of Public Information, United Tribes Technical Center

* Write to us and we will send information on this project

Fox Chapel Publishing , Box 7948 , Lancaster PA 17604

# NATIVE FOODS

America's first people were called "Indians" based on the mistaken belief of the explorers that they had reached India. This lack of understanding and cultural arrogance would be a dominant theme in Native History.

The only knowledge many people have of America's first people is based on the legend of the first Thanksgiving among the early settlers and the fiction of Hollywood movies. Outside these sources, knowledge of Native Indians and their culture and traditions is sorely lacking. Few people have an appreciation for the variety and complexity of the different cultures that were in existence in North America long before the coming of the white man.

The different groups of North American native people had developed advanced farming techniques, distinctive craftsmanship and the fine arts and music characteristic of thriving, vibrant societies.

Native Indians left a great legacy of foodstuffs and cultivation practices. Corn, now a food staple world-wide was hardly known in Europe at the time of the settlers. However, Indian tribes had been cultivating corn for centuries and developed a great deal of knowledge and technical expertise. Early explorers reported sighting corn fields over 18 miles long. Techniques of breeding pure and hybrid varieties of corn were well-known. Counting the work of different tribes, Indians had developed over 30 varieties of corn - bred for specific climatic areas and different culinary purposes. The Hopi Indians were particularly adept in this regard, having developed a corn plant which grew close to the ground with little stalk or leaf but large ears - ideal for the arid environment of the Southwest.

Equally advanced processing methods for corn were part of native culture. Only recently have scientists discovered that corn soaked in ashes and water converts into a foodstuff most easily digested by the human body. This process was practiced for hundreds of years by the Indians of the Southwest. Many varieties of corn had hulls too thick to eat. The Indians manufactured lye from wood ashes, using the lye to dissolve the hulls away, leaving *hominy* - a later variation of which became that classic of the American South - *grits*. Dr. Kellogg's discovery that hominy could be toasted and flattened formed the basis for the company bearing his name and for the modern breakfast cereal industry.

The Indians also taught the first white men how to dry and use red peppers, make maple syrup, use wild plants and herbs and appropriate method of preserving meat. It is ironic that such famous "All American" foods as Boston Baked Beans. New England Clam Bake, succotash, chili, crackerjacks, doughnuts and pumpkin pie are all based on Native Indian Recipes.

In addition to the all-important introduction of corn to the rest of the world, the Indians also demonstrated the value and usefulness of potatoes, tomatoes, squash, avocado, sweet potatoes, tapioca and wild rice to the early settlers.

There are few items that really qualify as snacks or candy in native cookery. Nuts and berries were gathered and eaten fresh or dried for later use. Some tribes carried an early version of Trail Mix which combined nuts, jerky, dried fruits and/or berries. Pumpkin seeds, squash seeds and sunflower seeds were salted and baked. Pinon seeds were roasted and salted (these are a very expensive snack now). Parched Corn resembles Cornnuts and is an interesting variation on popcorn.

Beverages did not play a major role in Indian cuisine. Teas were brewed from a variety of herbs which varied according to the region in which the tribe resided. Most tribes used herbal teas for a variety of medicinal purposes . These are outside the scope of this book.

The spices and seasoning used in these recipes are mostly modern rather than the authentic but obscure and difficult-to-obtain original ingredients.

Prior to the coming of the settlers, Native Americans obtained meat for their diets by hunting and fishing. Most tribes believed that animals had souls which could communicate with other wildlife even after they were killed. Because of this belief, many detailed rituals were developed for the hunting, killing and eating of game. It was thought that if an animal's body was treated with respect, it would send positive message to other animals. As a consequence of this, elaborate ceremonies praised the beauty, valor and goodness of the kill. Were the animal's spirit to be insulted, it would warn other game to flee the hunters. Many hunters asked the Creator for forgiveness before killing an animal.

Since some tribes believed gods appeared on earth in the form of animals such as snakes and rabbits, they were not eaten. Other tribes also believed that young braves could not eat of their first kill without bringing themselves permanent bad luck at hunting.

Provisions were also made in many tribes so that it was not only the best hunters whose families ate. While the brave who brought down the kill was allowed to select the prime parts, the member of the hunting party who touched the animal second was entitled to the rest. Visitors to an Indian dwelling were fed during their visit so the homes of the best hunters became very popular places during times when food was scarce. Obtaining enough food during the seasons when game was near and abundant posed no difficulties.

During the winter months, however, hunting parties frequently had to journey large distances to find the meat they required. Eventually the European demand for furs and pelts so seriously depleted the available supply of game that hunting became an extremely taxing pursuit.

The recipes that follow benefit from the characteristic taste of wild game. However, these recipes may also be utilized with domesticated meat and poultry.

# OVEN TIMES AND TEMPERATURES

|  | TIME PER POUND | TEMPERATURE |
|---|---|---|
| **GAMEBIRDS** | | |
| Ducks | 15 minutes | 350 F |
| Goose | 25-30 minutes | 325-350 F |
| Partridge | 18-20 minutes | 350F |
| Pheasant | 15 minutes | 325 F |
| Pigeon | 18-20 minutes | 350 F |
| Quail | 15 minutes | 350 F |
| | | |
| **BIG GAME** | | |
| Bear | 30-35 minutes | 325-350 F |
| Moose | 30-35 minutes | 325-350 F |
| Deer | 15-20 minutes | 300-325 F |
| | | |
| **SMALL GAME** | | |
| Beaver | 25-30 minutes | 300-325 F |
| Ground Hog | 25 minutes | 300-325 F |
| Muskrat | 25 minutes | 300-325 F |
| Porcupine | 25 minutes | 300 F |
| Squirrel | 20-25 minutes | 325 F |
| Raccoon | 15 minutes | 300 F |
| Rabbit | 20 minutes | 300-325 F |
| | | |
| **FISH** | | |
| All Fish | 20 minutes | 325-350 F |

# VI.

# USEFUL TIPS

*Simmer a pan of vinegar on the stove when cooking any food that has a strong odor. This will help dispel this odor.

*Dip your spoon in cold water when spooning dumplings or drop biscuits. This prevents the dough from sticking.

*Thaw fish in milk. The milk draws out the "frozen" taste and provides a fresh caught taste.

*To remove scales from fish, nail some bottle caps on a piece of board, and use them to scrape the fish.

*To remove the gamey taste from beaver, add a tablespoon of coffee to the water when parboiling.

*Submerging a lemon in hot water for 15 minutes before squeezing, will make it yield almost twice as much juice.

*Wild, leafy edibles have a longer life span if stored in paper rather than cellophane bags.

*Buffalo meat is not wild or gamey tasting. While beef may be red in color, buffalo is a much darker color, almost brown.

*Buffalo is approximately 30% higher in protein than beef and contains almost no cholesterol due.

*In cooking buffalo, the best way to serve it is in the rare to medium range of doneness. This meat will become tough if overcooked.

*When cooking the snapping turtle; after removing the head, be very careful not to touch the head for at least 24 hours, as the nerves remain alive for at least that amount of time.

*When cooking large game, never put salt on before cooking; salt makes the meat tough.

*For marinating any game meat, always use a dry wine (never sweet).

*When roasting game birds, add a carrot to absorb the grease in the roasting pan.

*All game birds are delicious when cooked with fruit (pineapple, oranges, cherries, etc.).

*The slower game birds are cooked: the better the taste will be.

*When a bird is well cooked, its flesh will come away easily from the bones.

# 3.

## ·CHAPTER ONE·
## BIG GAME COOKERY
### DEER, MOOSE, ELK, BUFFALO, BEAR

# DEER

Deer, as well as other big game animals, will taste better when killed properly with a good clean quick shot. A poorly placed shot will cause the animal to suffer pain and stress. This causes a chemical reaction in the meat, giving it a stronger, gamier taste. Venison has a delicious, distinctive flavor, and is very healthy - containing one third the calories of an equivalent serving of beef.

The difference in taste between deer also depends heavily on their diet. A swamp buck will have a much stronger taste than a corn-fed deer. If necessary, we recommend marinading to sweeten the taste of any game meat.

See recipes that follow as well as the " **Sauces, Marinades ...**" section.

# WHITETAIL DEER

The Whitetail Deer is the most plentiful big game animal found in North America , with a population numbering in the millions. The typical whitetail stands 36-40 inches high at the shoulder . Average weight is 150 pounds with record-breakers tipping the scales at 400 pounds plus.

The whitetail is named for its characteristic *flag* - the white underside of its tail which shows when raised in flight. Whitetails range from the southern edge of the coniferous forest in Canada all the way south into Mexico. Rarely found in the arid areas of the American west.

# MULE DEER /BLACKTAIL DEER

Mulies and blacktails lack the distinctive swept forward rack of the whitetail. The mule deer is somewhat heavier than the whitetail and stands taller - 40-42 inches at the shoulder. *Mulies* - named for their mule-like ears, range from the Pacific coast east to Texas / Minnesota, north to Alaska and south into Mexico.

The blacktail is a smaller cousin of the mule deer, being smaller and lighter even than the typical whitetail. Blacktails are found primarily in a narrow region running along the Pacific coast from Alaska to central California.

# VENISON RIBS AND SAUCE

*5 lbs. venison ribs*                              *2 tbsp. salt*
*Brine made from 1 part vinegar*          *1 onion, sliced*
*to 3 parts water*                                *melted margarine*

*2 bay leaves*

## *RIB SAUCE:*

*1 1/2 cups water*                                *2 tbsp. lemon juice*
*1 cup chili sauce*                               *1/2 tsp. chili powder*
*1/4 cup steak sauce*                            *1/2 tsp. salt*

Make enough brine from vinegar and water to cover ribs. Add bay leaves, salt and onions. Marinate for 48 hours in refrigerator. Drain and pat dry. Place ribs in a shallow pan and brush ribs with melted margarine. Roast for 30 minutes at 450 F. Baste once again with margarine and reduce heat to 350 F. In saucepan combine sauce ingredients and bring to a boil over medium heat. Pour rib sauce over the ribs and bake for 1 1/2 to 2 hours, basting often.

# VENISON SHEPHERD'S PIE

| | |
|---|---|
| 1 1/2 lbs. ground venison | 1 cup carrots, cooked |
| 1 onion, chopped | 1 cup peas |
| 4 tbsp. shortening | 3 cups potatoes, mashed |
| 1 cup beef gravy | margarine |

paprika

Melt shortening in a skillet and add onions. Cook onions until transparent. Add ground venison and fry until well browned. Drain. Pour venison and onion mixture into a 2 quart casserole dish. Mix in gravy. Add carrots and peas in alternate layers, then cover mixture with mashed potatoes. Dot with margarine, and sprinkle with paprika.

Bake at 400 F for 25 to 30 minutes.

## MEATBALL STEW

| | |
|---|---|
| 1 lb. ground venison | 1 (28 oz.) can tomatoes |
| 1 egg | 1 (19 oz.) can whole potatoes, drained |
| 1/2 tsp. salt | |
| pinch of garlic powder | 2 cups frozen carrots |
| pinch of basil | 1 tsp. basil |
| pinch of oregano | 1/2 tsp. oregano |
| pinch of pepper | salt and pepper to taste |
| 1 tbsp. vegetable oil | 2 tbsp. flour |

Beat egg in large bowl and mix in ground venison, salt and remaining seasonings. Mix thoroughly and shape venison mixture into 2 inch balls. Heat oil in a deep skillet and add meatballs. Cook until well browned and then remove from skillet. Pat excess grease from meatballs and drain skillet. Place meat in pot and sprinkle lightly with flour. Stir in tomatoes, vegetables, 1 teaspoon of basil, 1/2 teaspoon oregano, salt and pepper to taste. Reduce heat and simmer for 15 minutes.

## FROZEN DEER LIVER FRY

| | |
|---|---|
| | 1 tsp. basil |
| 1 lb. fresh deer live | 1/4 cup flour |
| 1/2 tsp. slat | 1/4 tsp. pepper |

Soak liver for two hours in salt water. Drain and pat dry. Freeze whole liver. Slice liver while frozen into thin slices. Dredge each slice in seasoned flour. Pan fry in oil over medium heat until tender.

# VENISON CURRY

3 tbsp. fat                                    1/2 cup raisins

2 cloves of garlic, minced

1 lb. venison shoulder, cut into 1 inch cubes

2 medium sized onions, sliced                  oil

1 tbsp. curry powder                           salt

1 cup tomatoes (canned)

Sear venison in hot oil. R emove from heat and set aside. In a heavy skillet heat 3 tablespoons of fat. When hot, add garlic and onions. Cook until lightly browned. Stir in curry powder. Add the tomatoes and raisins and simmer for 10 minutes. Add venison cubes to tomato mixture. Season with salt and simmer for 1 1/2 hours. Add water when necessary to maintain liquid level.

✳

# VENISON BALLS

2 lbs. ground venison              1/2 tsp. chili pepper

2 eggs, slightly beaten                1 oz. soy sauce

2 cups cooked rice              2 tbsp. hickory flavored barbecue
                                sauce

1 tsp. salt                            1/4 cup water

1/2 tsp. pepper                prepared spaghetti sauce

Mix together all ingredients and shape into balls. Lay balls in the bottom of a roasting pan and cover with spaghetti sauce. Bake at 325 F. until done.

# SCALLOPED VENISON
# AND POTATO DINNER

1 lb. ground venison

4 potatoes, peeled and sliced

salt and pepper

2 onions, peeled and sliced

2 cups spaghetti sauce

1 tbsp. brown sugar

1/4 cup grated cheese

1/4 cup crushed corn flakes

Arrange a layer of potatoes sliced in the bottom of a greased 8" baking dish. Sprinkle with salt and pepper, then add a layer of onions. Break up meat and spread over onions. Add remaining potatoes, then onions. Cover with spaghetti sauce. Sprinkle brown sugar over top. Cover and bake at 350 F for 30 minutes. Uncover and sprinkle cheese and corn flakes. Continue to bake for an additional 30 minutes.

# VENISON MEAT BALLS
# IN PEPPER SAUCE

1 lb. ground venison

1/2 lb. minced porl

2 eggs, well beaten

1/2 cup bread crumbs

1/4 cup milk

1 1/2 tsp. salt

1/4 tsp. savory

flour

3 tbsp. salad oil

2 garlic cloves minced

1 onion, sliced

1 green pepper, sliced

1 can mixed vegetables, undrained

1 tsp. beef extract

1 cup water

1 bay leaf

1 tsp. chili powder

2 tsp. chili peppers

Mix first seven ingredients together and shape into balls about 1 inch in diameter. Roll in flour. Heat salad oil in a skillet; pan fry meat balls until brown, then transfer to a deep saucepan. Reheat oil in skillet and add onion, garlic and green peppers. Cook till onion is transparent; then add remaining ingredients and simmer for 10 minutes. Thicken slightly if desired. Pour hot sauce over the meat balls and simmer for 15 minutes.

✳

# PICKLED VENISON HEART

*1 tsp. salt*
*1 venison heart*
*2 small bay leaves*
*1 onion, sliced*
*liquid to cover (3 parts water/1 part vinegar)*

Place heart in a large saucepan and add enough water to cover. Add salt and bay leaves. Bring to a boil, then reduce heat to simmer. Cover and cook until meat is tender. Drain, cool and slice heart thinly. Place slices in a bowl along with onion and water vinegar mixture (enough to cover meat pieces). Salt and pepper to taste. Refrigerate for 3 hours. Remove meat from water vinegar solution, pat dry and use in sandwiches like roast beef.

# BAKED VENISON HEART
# WITH ONIONS

*1 venison heart*
*2 tbsp. flour*
*2 1/2 cups stewed tomatoes*
*6 medium onions*

## STUFFING:

*1 cup bread crumbs*
*1 1/2 tsp. salt*
*1/2 tsp. sage*
*1/4 tsp. pepper*
*3 tbsp. margarine*
*2 tbsp. bacon fat*

Wash venison heart and remove large veins and arteries. Fill cavity left by removing veins with bread stuffing. Sew heart to hold stuffing in. Melt bacon fat in a frying pan and brown heart on all sides after rolling in flour. Place heart in a roasting pan and pour stewed tomatoes over it and group onions around. Cover and bake at 275 F for 3 hours.

# COOKED VENISON TONGUE

*1 fresh venison tongue*
*1 tsp. salt*
*pepper*
*1 onion, sliced*
*1 bay leaf*

Cover tongue with cold water and add remaining ingredients. Simmer until tongue is tender. Remove tongue from pot and cool slightly. Remove tissue and skin. Slice tongue and serve.

# VENISON BOILED TONGUE

*1 venison tongue*          *1/2 tsp. salt per pound of venison*
*juice of 1 lemon*                      *2 bay leaves*
*1 tbsp. mixed pickling spice*     *1/4 cup dry celery leaves*

Scrub tongue thoroughly and place in a pot and cover with boiling water. Add remaining ingredients. Bring to a boil and cook for another 2 hours. Remove skins and root ends. Serve with horseradish sauce. (See following).

# HORSERADISH SAUCE

4 tbsp. melted butter            6 tbsp. prepared horseradish
2 tbsp. flour                            1/4 tsp. salt
                    1 cup milk

In a saucepan, blend butter and flour until smooth.  Then gradually, stir in the milk. Last, stir in horseradish and salt and cook over medium heat until thickened.  Add salt and pepper to taste.

✳

# WILD GAME PIE

## CRUST:

2 cups flour                              1 egg
2 tbsp. baking powder            1 tsp. salt
2 tbsp. butter or margarine         milk

Mix together the dry ingredients.  Beat egg in some of the milk and add to dry ingredients.  Add enough milk to make the crust like a pie dough.  Divide in half and set aside.

5 lbs. moose or venison, cubed            2 onions, chopped
salt and pepper                                      1 tsp. cinnamon

In a small roast pan spread out 1/2 the cubed meat.  Salt and pepper meat.  Sprinkle 1 chopped onion and 1/2 tsp. cinnamon over meat. Roll out half of dough and cover the meat mixture. On top of this first piece of pastry spread the remaining meat cubes, salt and pepper.  Sprinkle remaining onion and cinnamon on top.  Cover with remaining rolled out pastry.  Bake at 250 F for 5 to 6 hours.

# SWEET AND SOUR POT ROAST

*2 tbsp. cooking oil*
*4 lbs. chuck roast (venison, moose)*
*1 cup chopped onion*
*1 tsp. salt*
*1/4 tsp. pepper*

*1/2 cup broth*
*1/3 cup cider vinegar*
*1/3 cup liquid honey*
*1 tbsp. cornstarch*
*1/4 cup water*

*1/2 tsp. dried thyme*

Heat oil in heavy saucepan.  Add meat and brown on all sides. Remove meat.  Add onion to hot oil, stirring constantly for 3 minutes. return meat to saucepan and sprinkle with salt, pepper and thyme. Add vinegar and broth then cover, and simmer for 2 hours. Add honey and continue simmering until tender, (approx. 1 hour more). Remove meat to hot platter. Bring liquid in saucepan to a full boil. Mix cornstarch and water together, then add to liquid gradually.  Stir until thickened and clear.  Turn down and simmer for 3 minutes.  Serve over meat slices.

## FIVE HOUR STEW

1 1/2 lb. venison
6 carrots, sliced
4 medium size potatoes, slice
1 tbsp. sugar
5 tbsp. minute tapioca

1 cup celery, chopped
1 onion, sliced
1 can tomatoes
1 can beef broth
2 tsp. salt

V8-brand vegetable cocktail

Put all ingredients into a large pot. Mix and cover with V8 juice plus 2 inches. Cover; simmer for 5 hours at 350 F. Stir occasionally.

✳

## MILLIES VENISON MEATBALLS

2 lbs. ground venison
2 cups soda crackers, crumbled

6 large onions, sliced
1 tsp. salt
4 cans tomato soup (10 oz)

1 tsp. pepper
2 eggs
1 cup water

Combine burger, soda crackers, salt, pepper and eggs. Mix thoroughly. Form into medium-sized meatballs. Brown well in a large heavy pot. Melt cooking fat in a large skillet. Saute onions until softened and slightly browned. Combine onions and tomato soup in a large pot with meatballs. Pour in 1 cup of water and mix thoroughly. Cover and simmer for 1 1/2 to 2 hours, stirring occasionally. Serve with whipped potatoes or just with Mom's Salad.

# CURRIED VENISON
# AND VEGETABLES

| | |
|---|---|
| 1 tbsp. vegetable oil | 1 lb. ground venison |
| 3 cups cabbage, shredded | 2 carrots, peeled and sliced |
| 2 stalks celery, sliced | 1 green pepper, cored and thinly sliced |
| 1 onion, peeled and chopped | 1 cup of broth |
| 1 1/2 to 2 tsp. curry powder | 1 1/2 tsp. salt |
| 1 tsp. of pepper | 1 1/2 cups macaroni |
| | 2 tbsp. parsley |

Heat oil in a cooking pot and brown the ground venison. Drain excess fat. Add cabbage, carrots, celery, green pepper and onions. Stir in broth and seasonings. Bring to a boil then reduce heat and simmer until vegetables are tender. Meanwhile, prepare macaroni as directed on the package. Drain and add macaroni to the broth and vegetable mixture. Garnish with parsley and serve.

✳

# MEATY TOMATO DUMPLINGS

*1 (10 oz.) can tomato soup*
*1 cup of water*
*1/2 cup tomato juice*

## DUMPLINGS:

*1 tbsp. salad oil*          *1 small onion, chopped*
*1/2 lb. ground venison*          *1 tsp. salt*
*1/4 tsp. garlic powder*          *1/4 tsp. sage*
*3/4 cups sifted pastry flour*          *1 tsp. baking powder*
*1 egg (well beaten)*          *2 tbsp. of milk*

Saute onion in oil until softened.  Add meat and seasonings.  Stir-fry gently until meat is cooked.  Remove from heat and cool slightly.

In a bowl, sift flour and baking powder together.  Add egg and milk and mix thoroughly; then mix in meat mixture.

Bring soup, water and tomato juice to a boil and add heaping spoonfuls of the dumpling mixture.  Cover and steam cook for 15 minutes.  Serves 4 people.

❋

# VENISON BROILED BURGERS

| | |
|---|---|
| 1 lb. ground venison meat | 2/3 cup soft bread crumbs |
| 1/4 cup minced onion | 2 tsp. horseradish |
| 4 tsp. salt | 1/4 tsp. sage |
| 1 tbsp. catsup or tomato juice | 1 tbsp. milk |

4 slices bacon

Mix bread crumbs, onion, horseradish, salt, pepper, sage, catsup and milk with ground meat. Shape into 4 patties. Wrap a piece of bacon around each patty and secure with toothpick. Broil each side until done, about 12 to 16 minutes.

✳

# HEAVENLY HASH

| | |
|---|---|
| 1 1/2 lbs. venison burger | 2 stalks of celery |
| 1 large onion | 3 cups of cooked macaroni |
| 1/2 cup grated cheese | 2 slices of bacon |
| 1 can of tomato soup | 1 can of mushroom soup (undiluted) |

Cook bacon crisp and set aside. Dice onion and celery. Brown meat, onion and celery in bacon drippings. Add macaroni to hamburg mixture. Add remaining ingredients including crumbled bacon. Place in casserole dish. Bake at 350 F for 45 minutes.

# EASY VENISON
# LIVER SKILLET

1 lb. venison liver                     1/4 cup all purpose flour

1/4 cup butter                          1 medium onion, sliced thinly

1 -19 oz. can tomatoes                  1 tsp. sugar

1 tsp. salt                             1 tsp. worcestershire sauce

1/4 tsp. basil or curry                 dash of pepper

1 1/2 cups of shredded cheddar cheese

    Cut liver into 1/2 inch strips and coat lightly with flour.  Melt butter in frying pan; add liver and brown quickly on both sides.  Add onion and fry gently until almost tender.  Stir in tomatoes, sugar, salt, worcestershire sauce, basil and pepper.

    Cover and simmer gently for approximately 15 minutes.  Add cheese and stir until melted.  If served in a casserole, garnish with additional cheese and broil until golden.  Serve alone or over boiled rice.

# FRIED VENISON LIVER

1 1/2 lbs. of venison liver, sliced
1/2 cup flour
1/2 tsp. salt

3 tbsp. lemon juice
1 tsp. basil
1/4 tsp. pepper

1 onion, grated
1 tsp. garlic powder
1/2 cup of bacon fat

2 eggs beaten
2 cups of dried bread crumbs
1/2 cup cream

Sprinkle lemon juice over the liver. Combine flour, basil, salt and pepper. Dredge liver slices completely. Mix together cream, onion, eggs and garlic. Dip the liver into this mixture and then dip again into dry bread crumbs. Fry quickly on both sides in hot bacon fat.

✳

# VENISON MEATBALLS
# AND MUSHROOMS

1 lb. ground venison
3/4 cup of bread or cracker crumbs
1/4 tsp. pepper
1 tsp. of celery salt

1 egg beaten
1/2 tsp. salt
3/4 tsp. nutmeg
1 cup of water

1 pkg. mushroom gravy mix

DIRECTIONS:

In a bowl, place meat and add all of the remaining ingredients. Mix well and then shape into balls. In a skillet brown meatballs over medium heat. Drain.

Place meatballs in a casserole dish and pour in mushrooms and liquid. Add 1 cup of water and 1 package of mushroom gravy mix. Cover and bake at 350 F for 1/2 hour.

✳

# PORCUPINES

| | |
|---|---|
| 1 lb. venison burger | 1/2 cup uncooked rice |
| 1/2 cup water | 1/3 cup onion, chopped |
| 1 tsp. salt | 1/2 tsp. celery salt |
| 1/8 tsp. garlic powder | 1/8 tsp. pepper |
| 1 can (15 oz.) tomato sauce | 1 cup water |
| 2 tsp. worcestershire sauce | |

In a bowl, mix burger, rice, 1/2 cup water, onion, salt, celery salt, garlic powder and pepper together. Form into balls. Cook meatballs in a skillet until brown, and then drain off the grease. Mix remaining ingredients and pour over meatballs. Heat to boiling and then reduce heat. Cover and simmer for 45 minutes (add more water during cooking if necessary).

✳

# MEATLOAF

| | |
|---|---|
| 1 1/2 lbs. ground venison | 1 cup quick rolled oats |
| 2 eggs, beaten | 1 cup milk |
| 1/4 cup onion, chopped | 2 tsp. salt |
| 1/4 tsp. pepper | 1 tsp. prepared mustard |
| 1 (10 oz. can) cream of mushroom soup, undiluted | |

Mix together all ingredients, except 1/2 can of the cream of mushroom soup and press into loaf pan. Use the remaining soup to pour on top of the meat loaf. Bake at 375 F for 1 hour.

✳

# GLAZED VENISON LOAF

| | |
|---|---|
| 2 lbs. ground venison | 1 cup dry bread crumbs |
| 4 tbsp. onion, grated | 1 tbsp. parsley |
| 1 cup sour cream | 2 eggs |
| 2 tbsp. worcestershire sauce | 1/2 cup tomato sauce |
| 1 tbsp. worcestershire sauce | 1 1/2 tsp. corn syrup |
| 1/2 tsp. salt | 1/4 tsp. pepper |

Mix together first 7 ingredients, and season with salt and pepper. Shape into a greased loaf pan and place in a 350 F oven for 45 to 50 minutes. When pan is cool turn meat out onto a baking sheet. Mix together tomato sauce, corn syrup and wocestershire sauce. Pour mixture over meat and bake for an additional 15 minutes.

# VENISON- BURGER
# CASSEROLE

1 lb. minced venison                    1 onion chopped

1 lb. macaroni                    1 lb. milk cheese, sliced thin

1 (10 oz. can) tomato soup, diluted with water

1/4 lb. margarine

1/2 cup green pepper, chopped


Saute onions and green pepper in 1 tablespoon of margarine. Brown ground venison with onion and pepper. Drain. Prepare macaroni according to package directions. Put macaroni in a large casserole; add hamburger, onion and pepper, stir in the tomato soup and cheese. Bake for 20 minutes at 350 F.

# SHIPWRECK DINNER

4 large potatoes, peeled and sliced thick    1 lb. minced venison

1 large onion, thinly sliced                    1/4 cup raw rice

1 cup celery chopped         1 (10 oz. can) tomato soup, diluted

margarine

DIRECTIONS:

In a greased casserole, put a layer of potatoes, a layer of onion and a layer of ground venison.  Sprinkle rice over the meat.  Distribute celery over the top and pour in the prepared tomato soup.  Dot with margarine, cover and bake at 325 F for 2 hours.

# CHILI CON CARNE

1 lb. venison burger

1 large onion, chopped

1 to 2 stalks of celery chopped

1 can of tomatoes

1 can tomato soup or paste

1 can kidney beans

1 to 2 tbsp. chili powder

garlic salt

salt and pepper

Brown burger in skillet and add onion and celery.  In a large pot add burger mixture and remaining ingredients and simmer 15 minutes.

# CHILARONI

1 lb. venison burger                    8 oz. tomato sauce
1 (10 oz. can) kidney beans      1 (28 oz. can) tomatoes
1 onion, chopped                      3 cups of macaroni cooked
2 tbsp. chili powder

Place burger and onions in a skillet and cook until meat is lightly browned.  Drain.  Add remaining ingredients to the skillet.  Simmer for 25 to 30 minutes.

✳

# VENISON CABBAGE ROLLS

1 large head of cabbage          1 1/2 lbs. ground venison
1 egg                                          1/2 tsp. salt
1/2 tsp. pepper                          1 cup cracker crumbs
1/4 cup catsup                           1/4 cup butter

DIRECTIONS:

Remove large leaves from cabbage.  Trim off thick part of each leaf.  Soak in boiling water for a few minutes so they become soft enough to roll.  combine burger, egg, salt, pepper, crackers and catsup.  Place mounds of meat mixture in each leaf.

Fold over sides of each leaf and roll.  Place in a dutch oven with melted butter and cook over medium heat until browned.  Then add water, so the rolls are covered.  Bring to a boil.  Then reduce heat and simmer for 1 hour.  Take out cabbage rolls and make gravy using flour and spice to taste.  Serve rolls covered with gravy.

✳

# VENISON POT ROAST WITH WILD CRANBERRIES

*3 lb. venison roast*  
*2 tbsp. fat*  
*2 cups raw cranberries*  
*1/2 cup celery, diced*  
*6 sprigs parsley*  

*flour*  
*3 cups boiling water*  
*1/2 cup onions, diced*  
*1 large bay leaf*  
*2 whole cloves*  

*1 1/2 tsp. salt*

Wash and pat meat dry.  Sprinkle meat with a little flour and then brown on all sides in heated fat. Add all the remaining ingredients except salt.  Cover and bring to a boil, then simmer for 2 1/2 hours.  Add salt and turn meat over in gravy.  If necessary, thicken gravy before serving.  Serves 6.

# QUICK MEAT PIE

| | |
|---|---|
| 1 (10 oz. can) tomato soup | 3/4 cup water |
| 1/4 tsp. rosemary | 1/8 tsp. pepper |
| 1 tsp. garlic powder | 2 cups cooked venison, cubed |

1 medium onion, chopped
1 (16 oz can) diced carrots, drained
1 (16 oz. can) whole potatoes, drained
1/2 cup cheddar cheese
pastry for 1 pie crust

Combine tomato soup and water and add the seasonings. Mix in cubed venison, onion, potatoes and carrots. Pour mixture into an ungreased baking dish and mix in cheese. Cover with pastry and seal at edges. Make two slits in center of pastry to allow steam to escape. Bake at 425 F for 20 minutes.

# VENISON AND NOODLES

3/4 lb. lean venison steak
  cut into thin strips
1/4 tsp. pepper
1/4 cup lemon juice
1/3 cup gingersnap crumbs
4 1/2 cups broad egg noodles

1 tbsp. margarine
1/2 cup chopped onion
1 1/4 cup homemade beef broth
1/4 tsp. cloves
1 tbsp. brown sugar
2 tbsp. margarine

2 tsp. poppy seeds

In a large skillet brown steak in 1 tablespoon of margarine. Add onion and pepper and cook until onion is tender. Add broth and lemon juice. Stir and add cloves. Bring to a boil and stir in gingersnap crumbs and brown sugar.

Simmer, uncovered for 15 to 20 minutes or until sauce thickens. Meanwhile, cook noodles as directed on package. Drain. Toss hot noodles with 2 tablespoons of margarine and poppy seeds. Pour meat mixture over noodles and serve.

# SPICED VENISON POT ROAST

4 tsp. whole cloves                    4 tsp. allspice
1/4 tsp. whole black pepper            1 tsp. salt
1/2 tsp. ground nutmeg                 1/2 tsp. ground mace
1 - 3 to 4 lbs. venison roast          2 tbsp. brown sugar
2 tbsp. vinegar                        2 tbsp. lard
                    1/4 cup of flour

Coarsely crack cloves, allspice and peppers. Mix with salt, nutmeg and mace. Rub spices over meat and press in. Place meat in a shallow dish. Combine sugar, vinegar and 1/4 cup water. Pour over meat and refrigerate overnight. turn meat often. Remove meat and reserve the marinade. In a dutch oven, brown meat in hot lard.

Add marinade and 1/2 cup of water. Cover and cook until tender, approx. 2 hours. Add more water if needed. Remove meat to warm platter and strain the juices remembering to skim off fat. Add water to make 1 1/2 cups of fluid, slowly blend 1/2 cup cold water into flour. Stir into juices. Cook and stir until thick. Cook 1 minute more. Season to taste. Serve auce with roast.

✳

# BRAISED VENISON
# WITH VEGETABLES

2 lbs. steak, cut about 1 inch thick          1 tsp. salt
1/4 tsp. pepper                                              flour
1/4 cup corn oil                              2 cups tomato juice
1 (12 -20 oz. can) whole kernel corn
1 (12 - 20 oz. can) green beans

Cut meat into 6 serving pieces. Sprinkle with salt and pepper and dredge in flour. Brown meat in hot corn oil over medium heat. Pour tomato juice over meat. Cover and simmer for 45 minutes. Add vegetables and simmer for 15 minutes longer. Makes 6 servings.

✳

# VENISON MINCEMEAT

1 quart apple cider

2 cups seedless raisins

1 cup dried cooked currants

3 greening apples, peeled, cored and
   chopped

1 cup chopped suet

2 tsp. salt

2 tsp. cinnamon

2 tsp. ginger

1 tsp. cloves

1 tsp. nutmeg

1/2 tsp. allspice

2 lbs. ground venison

Place the cider, raisins current, apples, and suet in a large heavy kettle. cover, and simmer for 2 hours.  Stir in remaining ingredients and simmer, uncovered for 2 hours, stirring occasionally.  Use as pie filling.

*

# FRIED OR BOILED INDIAN SAUSAGE

Use tripe (boiled previously) inside out, about half a foot in length. Fill this with dried meat, grease, and fry until it is crisp. then slice into pieces to serve.

# TRIPE SPECIAL

Select the straight intestine of a cow. With the two ends open, turn the intestine inside out. Place cubes of fresh beef, salt and pepper seasoning in the tube. Fasten each end of the intestine with string. Boil the sausage for an hour; then it is ready to serve.

✳

# VENISON AND WILD RICE STEW

*3 1/2 lbs. venison*　　　　　　*2 cups apple cider*
*6 cups water*　　　　　　　　*2 onions, quartered*
*2 tsp. salt*　　　　　　　　　*1/8 tsp . pepper*
*1 1/2 cup wild rice, washed*

Marinate venison cut into 2" cubes in apple cider for two hours in large kettle. Add water, onions, and seasonings. Simmer, uncovered, for 3 hours or until venison is tender. Add wild rice, cover and simmer for 20 minutes. Stir, then cook uncovered 20 minutes more until rice is tender and most of liquid is absorbed.

# VENISON CHILI

| | |
|---|---|
| *2 lbs. venison* | *flour* |
| *1/4 cup oil* | *2 onions, chopped* |
| *2 cloves garlic, minced* | *8 oz. canned green chilis* |
| *4 green tomatoes, cubed* | *1 tsp. salt* |
| *1 tsp. cumin* | *1/2 tsp. oregano* |

Cut venison into one inch cubes, dredge in flour and brown in heavy kettle, remove to plate and saute onions, garlic, and chilli peppers in oil until slightly wilted.

Return meat to pan with remaining ingredients and enough water to cover and simmer for 2-3 hours or until meat is tender.

✳

# VENISON STUFFED PEPPERS

| | |
|---|---|
| 6 green peppers | 2 1/2 cup cooked venison |
| 6 mushrooms | 2 scallions, sliced |
| 1/4 cup bacon drippings | 1 tsp. salt |
| | 1/4 tsp. pepper |

Wash and core peppers.  Saute remaining ingredients in bacon drippings.

Stuff peppers with venison mixture and bake at 350 F. for 45 minutes.

# VENISON STEAK

4 venison steaks
2 shallots, shopped
2 carrots, sliced
2 onions, chopped
1/8 tsp. thyme

1/4 tsp. pepper
2 cups apple cider
1 cup white vinegar
1 clove garlic, minced
1/2 cup oil

2 bay leaves

Marinate steaks cut 1/2" to 3/4" thick in marinade made of remaining ingredients except oil for 24 hours.  Remove steaks from marinade and dry.

Put marinade in small saucepan and cook it and vegetables until tender and sauce equals approximately 1/2 cup.  Saute the steaks in shallow, hot fat until brown on both sides. Steaks will be rare. Serve sauce over steak.

# BAKED
# VENISON HEART

*1 3/4 lb. venison heart*
*1 1/2 tbsp melted butter*
*2 cups soft bread crumbs*
*dash of pepper*
*1/2 tsp. sage*
*1 tbsp. onion, finely chopped*
*2 tbsp. shortening*
*1/4 tsp. salt*
*1 1/2 cup boiling water*

Wash heart in warm water to remove blood. Combine butter, bread and seasonings and stuff heart. Skewer together. Sear in hot shortening, until browned on all sides.

Place in rack on roaster, add boiling water , also drippings from searing. Cover and bake at 325 F for 2 1/2 hours.

✳

# MEATBALLS

1 lb. ground venison                    1 lb. ground pork

2 cups of bread crumbs                       2 eggs

1/2 cup chopped onion                   2 tbsp. parsley

1 small green pepper, chopped


SAUCE:

1/2 cup barbecue sauce      1 (10 oz.) jar apricot or peach jam


Combine venison, ground pork, bread crumbs, eggs, onion, parsley and chopped green pepper. Form into balls and place 1 inch apart on cookie sheet. Bake in the oven at 325 F for 30 minutes.

Mix barbecue sauce and jam and pour over meatballs. Bake in 350 F oven for 30 minutes longer. Makes 4 to 5 dozen. Can be served as an appetizer or may be served as a main course.

✳

# UPSIDE DOWN
# BURGER PIE

| | |
|---|---|
| *1 single pie crust, unbaked* | *3/4 lb. ground venison* |
| *1 small onion, chopped* | *1 can tomato soup* |
| *1/4 cup shortening* | *2/3 cup milk* |
| *1 1/2 cups flour* | *3 tsp. baking powder* |
| *1 tsp. salt* | |

Saute ground venison and onion until meat is browned.  Drain. Add soup and set aside.  Combine dry ingredients and cut in shortening. Mix in the milk, all at once.  Knead until smooth.  Roll out on a floured board in a circle large enough to cover a pie plate.  Cover with pie crust and bake at 375 F for 15 to 20 minutes or until done.

# VENISON OVEN STEW

| | |
|---|---|
| *2 lbs. cubed venison* | *1 small tin mushrooms and liquid* |
| *1 (28 oz. can) tomatoes* | *1 (10 oz. can) tomato soup* |
| *1/2 soup can water* | *2 medium onions, diced* |
| *salt and pepper* | *pinch of garlic* |
| *6 to 8 potatoes* | |

Stir all ingredients, except potatoes, into a small roasting pan. Cover and cook for 1 1/2 hours at 350 F.

Add potatoes and cook for 20 to 30 minutes longer.

# BUFFALO

The buffalo was the mainstay of the Plains Indians, providing food, clothing , tools and shelter.  Buffalo and the buffalo hunt is a prominent feature of many  ceremonies and religious beliefs.

As many as 50 million buffalo roamed the North American continent at their peak.  As a matter of government policy, almost all were destroyed in the process of bringing the tribes into submission and relegating them to reservations.

# THE MANY USES OF BUFFALO

| | |
|---|---|
| Hide scraper | Bones |
| Needles | Small Bones |
| Spoon | Horn |
| Bow String | Muscle |
| Moccasins | Hide |
| Kettle | Stomach |
| Paint brush | Nose Bone |
| Cooking Oil | Tallow |
| Arrow Points | Bones |
| Digging Tool | Shoulder Blade |
| Bowl | Skull |
| Berry Pounder | Leg Bone |

The most important tools used on the buffalo, were the scraper, the flesher, and the drawsblade.

The scraper was a flat stone which was used to remove the meat and fat from the inside of the hide.

The flesher was a piece of flint with a handle. It was used to hack down the hide to the required thickness.

The drawsblade was a curved willow stick filled with a bone splinter. It was used to shave the hair from the hide.

# TANNING

Tanning the hide was considered by the Indians as women's work. The brains and liver of the buffalo were mixed with soapweed and grease and rubbed into both sides of the hide. After this mixture was allowed to soak into the hide overnight, it was then dried by the sun.

# BLACKFEET PEMMICAN

Buffalo, cut in thin strips, was dried for the winter in much the same way jerky was. The meat, once dried was crushed into powder on flat rocks. Pemmican was used in soups, mixed with crushed berries (usually cherries or buffalo berries) and melted fat, and was frequently carried in leather pouches on journeys.

*5 cup dried meat (pemmican)*
*3 cups mashed berries*
*1/4 cup shortening*
*1/4 cup sugar*

Mix ingredients together in large bowl and serve. Cinnamon may be added for extra flavor.

NOTE: Pemmican was a staple among the Plains Indians and probably was the idea from which mincemeat sprang. The Pueblos varied the process slightly by using venison rather than buffalo and by using apricots or dried wild plums in place of berries.

# PLAINS INDIAN PEMMICAN

Grind chokeberries, pits included. Add same amount of dried buffalo meat, pounded or ground fine. Mix meat and chokeberries with melted buffalo tallow, enough to hold mixture together and form into flat patties. Dry, these patties may be carried on trips away from camp. They are very nutritious.

## BUFFALO POZOLE

| | |
|---|---|
| 2 tbsp. oil | 2 large onions, chopped |
| 3/4 lb. mushrooms | 1 lb. buffalo |
| 2 can tomatillos | 1 can hominy, drained |
| 1 can baby corn | 1/4 cup cilantro, chopped |
| 5 dried red hot chilies | salt and pepper |

Saute onion and mushrooms in oil in large kettle for 20 minutes. Pour mixture out of pan and set aside. Stir in buffalo, fry until browned and crumbly. Add remaining ingredients and simmer gently for 30 minutes. Chilies may be removed and discarded if desired.

## BUFFALO STEW

| | |
|---|---|
| 2 lbs. buffalo | 1/4 cup oil |
| 2 cups dried corn | 2 large onions, chopped |
| 2 cloved garlic, minced | 1 tsp. oregano |
| 3 carrots, sliced | 12 juniper berries |
| 2 potatoes, cubed | 8 cups water |
| 1 green pepper, sliced | 1 tsp. salt, 1/4 tsp. pepper |

Cut buffalo into 1" cubes and brown in oil. Remove to a plate and saute onions and garlic in meat oil. Return meat to pan and add water and seasoning. Cook 2 hours or until meat is tender. Add remaining vegetables and cook until done, approximately 30 minutes.

Buffalo was the meat of choice for Plains tribes. Cooked much as we now cook beef, it was roasted, stewed, dried, bones formed the basis of soups. One of the most important celebrations was the Feast of the First Buffalo.

# JERKY INFORMATION

4 pound slab of meat produces 1 pound of jerky.

Jerky is 75% protein

Recommended as a light source of protein for hiking and canoe trips.

Nobody should go into the bush without it. It's a survival food and tastes delicious.

Original jerky was rubbed down with salt and hung in tepees to smoke and dry.

French explorers yanked and pulled at the meat while it was hanging to speed up the drying process, hence the translated name "Jerked Beef".

To eat, simply chew like gum; keep going, the flavor improves.

# BUFFALO JERKY

*1 pkg. instant meat marinade*

*1 3/4 cup cold water*

*1/2 tsp. liquid smoke*

*1/4 tsp. garlic powder*

*1/4 tsp. onion powder*

*1/4 tsp. black pepper*

*1/2 tsp. tabasco sauce*

*1 1/2 - 2 lbs. buffalo meat in strips 6" x 1/2" w. x 1/2" t.*

Place meat in container and cover with marinade, piercing meat slices deeply with fork. Marinate overnight in a covered container in fridge. Remove meat strips, drain slightly and place on rack making sure strips do no overlap. Place a cookie sheet under the rack in a 150 - 175 F. oven and bake 3 -3 1/2 hours.

Remove from oven; cool, and store in a covered container in fridge. These larger pieces are not dried long and will be soft. Meat must be refrigerated to protect from spoilage.

# GREAT HUMPED BACK ROAST

*3 -5 lbs. chuck or brisket*
*roast*
*garlic slivers*

*2 cups strong black coffee*
*2 cups water*
*salt and pepper to taste*

*onion slivers*
*1 cup vinegar*

Using a large knife, cut slits completely through the meat.  Insert slivers of garlic down into the slits.  Onion may be substituted if you  don't care for garlic, or both, if you like.  Pour 1 cup of vinegar over the meat, making sure it runs down into the slits.  Put this in refrigerator and leave it for 24 to 48 hours.

When ready to cook, place roast in a big, heavy pot and brown in oil until nearly burned on all sides.  Pour 2 cups strong black coffee over the meat.  Add 2 cups water and cover.

Simmer on top of stove for 4 - 6 hours.  Season with salt and pepper approximately 20 minutes before serving.

Guaranteed to fall apart at the touch of a fork, no matter how tough your meat originally was.

The gravy may be thickened or just left as is.

# BUFFALOAF

2 lbs. buffalo burger
1 cup fine dry bread
   crumbs
1 tsp. salt, dash pepper
1/2 tsp. fine herbs

3 eggs
1 cup milk
1 cup shredded carrot
finely chopped onion and
   celery to taste

1/4 tsp. nutmeg
1/2 cup hickory - flavored catsup

Place in bowl; bread crumbs, salt, pepper, herbs and nutmeg. Add eggs, milk and beat well. Let stand a few minutes.

Gently blend in burger, carrot, onion and celery. Spread evenly in a 9 x 13 inch pan; spread catsup evenly over the meat mixture.

Bake at 325 F. for 1 hour or until done. Let stand about 5 minutes before cutting.

✳

# TUCKER'S STEW
# FOR AN ARMY

2 large sized buffalo                Brown gravy (lots)
2 rabbits (optional)                 Salt and pepper to taste

Cut buffalo into bite-sized pieces, (this will take about 2 months, so start early). Reserve the heads and tails as you will need something to store the pieces in.

After it is all cut up, put in a large pot and add enough brown gravy to cover the meat.

Vegetables, etc. may be added at this time to taste. Cook stew over a kerosene fire about 4 weeks at 400 F. Periodically add water and stir.

This will serve about 3937 people. If more guests are expected, the 2 rabbits may be added, but do this only if necessary as most people do not like fine hare in their stew.

# ELK, (WAPITI)

The elk (Shawnee Indian name - Wapiti) is the second largest antlered animal in North America after the moose. Bull elks stand about 60 inches high at the shoulder and typically weigh 600-800 pounds with record breakers weighing 1200 pounds plus. The cow is somewhat smaller, weighing in the vicinity of 450-600 pounds.

The range of the elk has diminished over the years. Predominantly, elk are now found in areas of Manitoba and Saskatchewan, the Rocky Mountains, northern Pacific coast and the Black Hills of South Dakota. Truly a regal animal in appearance, the bugle call of a bull elk is never forgotten.

# ELK STEW WITH

# ACORN DUMPLINGS

| | |
|---|---|
| *4 pieces bacon, chopped* | *1 1/2 lbs. elk meat* |
| *1 quart water* | *1 onion, chopped* |
| *1 tsp. salt* | *2 bay leaves* |
| *3 potatoes, diced* | *2 carrots, sliced* |
| *1/4 cup acorn meal* | *1/2 cup cold water* |

Cut meat into 1" cubes, brown meat with bacon, add water, salt, onions, and bay leaves. Cover and simmer 2 hours or until meat is tender. Add vegetables and cook 30 minutes longer. Combine acorn meal with 1/2 cup water and stir into simmering stew. Top with Acorn Dumplings.

## Dumplings:

| | |
|---|---|
| *1/2 cup acorn meal* | *1/2 cup whole wheat flour* |
| *1 1/2 tsp. baking powder* | *2 tbsp. milk* |
| *2 tbsp. oil* | *1 egg beaten* |

Combine dumpling ingredients and beat until smooth. Drop by spoonfuls on simmering stew. Cover and steam 12 to 15 minutes.

# MADBEAR S

# ELK STEW

*2 cups rice*
*12 dried wild turnips*
*7 wild onions (dice green onion tops)*
*one lb. dried elk meat*

Soak dried turnips for one hour . Use a large kettle for the stew.  Let the turnips and dried meat simmer for two hours.   Then add the onions, green tops and rice.  Add salt and pepper , seasoning.

Boil for ten minutes, cover and then let the stew simmer for five minutes.  The stew is then ready to serve.

✳

# SPICY ELK MEAT BALLS

| | |
|---|---|
| *1 lb. ground meat* | *2 tbsp. chopped green pepper* |
| *1 tbsp. grated onion* | *1/2 tsp. garlic salt* |
| *1/2 tsp. celery salt* | *2 cups tomato juice* |
| *2 whole cloves* | *1/2 tsp. cinnamon* |
| *1 tbsp. worcestershire sauce* | *1 tbsp. honey* |
| *1/2 cup wild rice* | |

Combine first five ingredients.  Form into balls about 1 inch  in diameter.  Heat next five ingredients in large covered skillet.

Add meatballs rolled in raw rice.  Cover and simmer 50 to 60 minutes.  Serve over wild rice. Makes five servings.

# SAVOURY STEW
# OF ELK

| | |
|---|---|
| 3 tbsp. bacon fat | 3 lbs. elk, cubed |
| 5 potatoes, cubed | 6 carrots, sliced |
| 1 1/2 cup celery, chopped | 1/2 lb. mushrooms, sliced |
| 2 cloves garlic, minced | 1 quart water |
| 1 tsp. salt | 1/4 tsp. pepper |
| 2 onions, chopped | 1/2 tsp. oregano |

Cut venison into 1" cubes, brown in bacon fat, remove meat to plate and saute onions and garlic in fat until translucent, add water, spices, and meat and cook 2 1/2 hours until tender. Add vegetables and cook until vegetables are done.

# WAPITI WILD RICE STEW

| | |
|---|---|
| 3 1/2 lbs., elk shoulder cut into 2 in. cubes | 2 tsp. salt |
| 2 onions, peeled and quartered | 1/8 tsp. fresh ground pepper |
| | 1 1/2 cups wild rice, washed |
| 2 qts. water | |

Place the meat, water and onions in a large heavy kettle and simmer, uncovered, for 3 hours, or until tender.

Mix in other ingredients, then simmer uncovered for about 30 minutes more until rice is tender. Stir frequently. Serve with fried bread and honey.

# MOOSE

The moose is the largest antlered mammal on earth weighing as much as 1800 lbs., and being on the average, 7 1/2 ft. tall to the shoulder. They are long legged and have a high hump shaped body which is dark brown in color. For their size, the moose is a very quiet animal with an extremely well developed sense of smell and hearing. They spend a good deal of time in the water and are excellent swimmers, even over long distances.

The only threat to the moose, besides man, is wolves. Only in a very weakened condition can a wolf pack take advantage of this great animal. The moose is a territorial animal rarely leaving their five square mile range except perhaps in the mating season.

Their diet consists of foliage, grasses, and aquatic plants. Moose meat is highly recommended as a substitute for many other red meats.

The moose is called *moos* by the Algonqian tribes, *mos* by the Delawares and *monswa* by the Cree - all mean *he who strips off*, referring to the eating method characteristic of the moose.

# MOOSE STEAK WITH MUSHROOM SAUCE

| | |
|---|---|
| 1 large moose steak | 3 tbsp. tomato paste |
| 3 tbsp. bacon drippings | 1/2 cup water or sherry |
| 1/2 cup bouillon or consomme | 1 cup sliced mushrooms |
| 1 medium onion, chopped | 2 tbsp. flour |
| 1/2 tsp. garlic powder | 1/4 cup cream |

*dash of paprika*

Heat bacon drippings in large skillet and brown steak on both sides thoroughly. Add broth, onion, garlic and tomato paste diluted in 1/2 cup of water or sherry. Cover pan and simmer for 1 hour or until meat is tender. Remove steak from pan and keep hot. Add mushrooms to pan liquid; cover and simmer for 1 minute. Thicken with flour and water mixture. Dilute with cream. Heat thoroughly.

Taste for seasoning. Pour over steak and sprinkle with paprika.

# CURRIED MOOSE BURGERS

| | |
|---|---|
| 1 lb. ground moose | 2 onions, chopped |
| 4 tbsp. bacon dripping | 1/2 tsp. horseradish |
| 1 can tomato sauce, small | 1 1/2 tsp. curry powder |

Shape meat into patties. Fry in cooking oil, over medium heat until brown on both sides. Stir in remaining ingredients; cover and simmer for 5 minutes or until meat is well done. Turn meat once.

Serve with sauce covering the meat.

# MOOSE PEMMICAN

| | |
|---|---|
| 1 lb. moose meat, well trimmed | 2 tbsp. melted suet |
| 1/2 cup raisins | 2 tbsp. melted vegetable shortening |
| 3 dates | 1 tbsp. lemon juice |

Cut meat into thin slices and dry as for jerky in slow oven (175 - 200 F) for 4 to 5 hours. Put the dried meat through a coarse grinder, then pulverize it into a fine powder. Grind the raisins and dates together and work into the meat with a fork or fingers until thoroughly blended.

Combine the melted suet, shortening and lemon juice. Pour over the meat/fruit until the mixture will hold together. Shape into small patties. The Indian pemmican patty was about three inches in diameter and half an inch thick.

This is nourishing and keeps without refrigeration.

# WHITNEY POT ROAST

*This recipe comes from Ontario Canada, just outside magnificent Algonquin National Park*

| | |
|---|---|
| 4 lbs. moose steaks, 1/2 lb. each | salt, pepper and paprika |
| 4 large onions, sliced | 1/2 cup butter or oil |
| 1/2 cup wine vinegar | 2 garlic cloves, minced |
| 1 small can tomato paste and an equal amount of water | 1 tbsp. pickling spice, tied in a bag |
| | 3 bay leaves |

Place steaks in cold water overnight. The next day, pat dry, and season with salt, pepper and paprika. In a skillet, quickly brown steaks in butter or oil. Remove meat from skillet and set aside. Saute onion and garlic until transparent and add remaining ingredient. Place meat in a heavy roast pan and pour onion mixture over it. Cover and cook in a 350 F oven for 2 hours or until meat is tender. Remove spice bag and bay leaves. Thicken liquid with flour and water. Serve.

# 54.

## MOOSE STEAK

2 lbs. moose, caribou or bear steak
6 small onion, sliced
1 green pepper, chopped
2 tbsp. fat
1/2 tsp. salt

1/2 tsp. pepper
1/4 cup flour
1 clove garlic, chopped
1 cup tomatoes
1 cup peas

Season flour with salt and pepper. Dredge meat with seasoned flour. Brown meat on both sides in hot fat, remove from pan.

Saute green pepper and garlic in same fat until tender. Place pepper and garlic over meat. Place meat in pan; add onions and tomatoes. Simmer until tender (approximately 2 hours).

Shortly before the meat is cooked, add peas and more seasoning if necessary. Arrange on a platter with vegetables on top.

✳

## SWEET PEPPER MOOSE STEAK

1 large moose steak
1/2 tsp. salt
1/4 tsp. pepper
1/4 cup flour

### STUFFING:

3 cups bread crumbs                    3/4 cup onion, chopped
3/4 cup celery, chopped                    1/2 cup butter
1/2 tsp. paprika                    1 sweet green pepper, sliced
salt and pepper

Mix flour, salt and pepper together.   Combine stuffing ingredients, and spread evenly over steak.

Roll up and tie.  Set the roll in a greased roasting pan.  Cover and bake at 350 F for 1 hour.

# MOOSE STEAKS WITH RICE

1 lb. moose, cut into thin strips       salt and pepper to taste
2 tbsp. lard                    4 tbsp. water
2 onions, sliced                    1 tsp. soya sauce
1 clove garlic                    2 tsp. cornstarch
1/2 cup celery                    1 cup water

Melt lard and slowly brown moose strips over low heat.  Add onion, garlic and celery. Season with salt and pepper. Add 1 cup water and simmer, cover for 20 minutes.  Thicken with cornstarch, 4 tablespoons of water and soya sauce.  Simmer for 5 minutes longer.

Serve hot over boiled rice.

# MOOSE AND CABBAGE TURNOVERS

3 tbsp. butter

3/4 cup finely chopped onion

1 1/2 lbs. ground moose

4 cups grated cabbage

3/4 cup grated raw carrot

2 tsp. salt

1/4 tsp. pepper

1/4 tsp. mace

1/4 tsp. worcestershire sauce

2 tbsp. water

double pie crust dough

1 egg yolk

1 tbsp. water

Heat butter in a large saucepan. Add onions and cook gently until tender, about 5 minutes. Add meat and stir until all redness disappears. Add cabbage, carrots, salt, pepper, mace, worcestershire sauce and water. Cover and simmer for 15 minutes.

Uncover and continue cooking until the liquid cooks away. Meat should be moist but not wet. Cool.

### CRUST:

Roll out pastry and cut into 6 inch squares. Put 1/4 cup of meat mixture on each square. Moisten adjacent edges and fold over (in a triangle shape). Press edges together. Prick with a fork. Place on large cookie sheet or sheets. Beat egg yolks and water together and brush over tops of turnovers. Bake for 25 to 30 minutes, or until very well browned. Serve at once.

## DEEP DISH MOOSE PIE

| | |
|---|---|
| 2 lbs. moose meat, cubes | 5 medium potatoes, cubed |
| 1/2 cup flour | pastry for 1 single pie crust |
| 1 tsp. salt | 3 tbsp. cornstarch |
| 3 carrots, peeled and sliced | water |
| 2 onions, chopped | 1 cup turnips, cubed |

Combine the flour and salt; dredge cubed meat. Then brown meat in an oiled skillet. Add 4 cups of water and simmer for 2 hours. Add carrots, onions and turnips, when tender add potatoes. Add more water if necessary. Thicken with cornstarch and water. Pour into a baking dish. Cover with the pastry; make 2 slits in the center and bake at 350 F for 20 to 25 minutes.

❋

## MOOSE CHEESE LOAF

| | |
|---|---|
| 2 lbs. ground moose meat | 2 tsp. salt |
| 1 large onion, chopped | 1 tsp. pepper |
| 1 1/2 cups cheese, diced | 1 tsp. celery salt |
| 1 large green pepper, chopped | 1 tsp. paprika |
| 1 cup dry bread crumbs | 2 1/2 cups milk |

Combine all ingredients and mix thoroughly.
Place into greased loaf pans and bake at 350 F for 2 hours.

# THE BEAR

The color of the black bear varies from black, to all shades of brown. They are found mostly throughout all wooded areas of North America, and range in a radius of about 15 miles.

It is ordinarily an independent creature and man is its only threat.

Bears are very clean animals, grooming often. They tend to eat anything from ants to elk, and all kinds of vegetation. Generally, they weigh in at 200-300 lbs. and the meat of the young bear is delicious.

The bear is skinned and butchered much the same as the domestic cow. It is important that the pelt is not marred during the process, because of its value.

# ROAST BEAR

*3 lbs. roast bear*
*3 large onions*
*1 can pineapple slices, and juice*
*2 cups water*

Place roast in pan.  Pour water over meat then cover with pineapple slices.  Slice onions and place along side of roast.

Cover roast with aluminum foil and bake for 1 hour.  Add juice from pineapple to roast and continue cooking for 1 1/2 hours.

# PAN FRIED BEAR STEAK

4 bear steaks, 1 inch thick
1 onion, sliced
1/2 cup vinegar
1/2 cup water

1/2 cup vegetable oil
1 tbsp. pickling spice
1 tbsp. salt
1 tbsp. bacon fat

salt and pepper

Trim all fat from bear steak and wash in cold water. Place steaks in a glass bowl. Add onion, vinegar, oil, water and spices. Marinate for at least 24 hours in the refrigerator, turning frequently. Remove steaks, pat dry and fry over medium heat in a pan that has been rubbed with oil or fat. To prevent sticking turn often until done. Add a little more fat when necessary. Marinade is optional.

# BEAR CHOPS

6 medium bear chops
1 clove garlic, halved
2 tbsp. bacon fat
1 large onion, chopped

4 carrots, diced, cooked
4 tbsp. flour
4 tbsp. chili sauce
1/2 cup dry wine

salt and pepper to taste

Rub chops with halved clove of garlic. Melt bacon fat in a skillet and sear chops on both sides. Place the chops in a lightly greased baking dish. Saute the onions and carrots in skillet until onions are transparent. Mix in flour, chili sauce and wine. Cook until thickened. On top of each chop place equal amounts of carrot mixture. Pour 1 cup of water into the baking dish; cover with tin foil and bake at 375 F for 60 to 70 minutes or until tender.

✳

# ROAST BEAR
# IN RAISIN SAUCE

*3 to 4 lbs. bear roast*　　　　　*1 tbsp. flour*
*3 1/2 cups water*　　　　　　*1/2 tsp. salt*
*1 1/2 tsp. dry mustard*　　　*1/4 tsp. pepper*
*2 tbsp. lemon juice*　　　　*1/4 cup seedless*
*raisins*

Cut all fat from roast; place in a roasting pan and pour in 2 cups of water. Cover and roast for 2 1/2 hours at 350 F. Mix all dry ingredients in a sauce pan. Slowly mix in remaining water and lemon juice. Add raisins.

Cook over medium heat, stirring constantly until it reaches consistency of syrup. Pour over bear roast and continue to roast for 30 minutes, basting 2 to 3 times throughout the baking time.

Do not forget to check the
"Sauces, Marinades & Batters" section
in the back of this book for more special sauces.

## SPICED BEAR ROAST

4 lbs. bear rump roast  
salt, pepper and garlic powder  
1/3 cup flour  
8 medium onions  

3 tbsp. bacon fat  
1/4 cup prepared mustard  
3/4 cup catsup  
3 cups hot water  

Saute onions in bacon fat and spread evenly on bottom of a roast pan. Trim bear roast of all fat; wash and place in roast pan. Sprinkle with salt, pepper and garlic powder. Combine mustard and catsup and spread thickly over the roast. Roast at 350 F for 3 1/2 to 4 hours, basting frequently. Transfer meat to a hot platter and skim fat from drippings. Stir in 1/3 cup of flour until all the flour disappears and add 3 cups of boiling water. Cook and stir until thick for gravy.

✳

## BEAR POT ROAST

1  3-lb. bear roast  
1/2 tsp. salt  
1/4 tsp. pepper  
1/2 tsp. cinnamon  

3 tbsp. white vinegar  
1/2 cup sherry wine  
1 cup water  
flour  

garlic to taste

Wipe roast dry and rub well with flour. Sprinkle on salt, pepper, cinnamon and garlic. Place roast in a roasting pan. Add water, wine and vinegar. Cover and bake at 375 F allowing 25 to 30 minutes per pound.

## SWEET BEAR ROAST

3 to 4 lb. roast
1/2 cup pineapple juice or vinegar
3 tbsp. brown sugar

1 tbsp. dry mustard
1/2 cup catsup
2 cups water

Mix pineapple juice or vinegar, brown sugar, dry mustard and catsup together in a large bowl. Place roast into mix and cover the meat completely. Cover and let stand in refrigerator for 10 to 12 hours, turning occasionally. Remove roast from marinade and place in a roasting pan. Add 2 cups of water and leftover marinade to the pan.

Cover and roast at 350 F for 3 1/2 to 4 hours, basting occasionally.

＊

## BRAISED BEAR STEAK

2 lb. bear steak
1/2 tsp. salt
1/4 tsp. pepper
3/4 tsp. cinnamon

2 (10 oz.) cans tomato soup
1 can water
2 tsp. lemon juice
bacon fat

2 large onions, sliced

Pat steak dry. Brown meat on both sides in a large skillet with a small amount of bacon fat. Add onions, tomato soup, water and lemon juice. Sprinkle salt, pepper and cinnamon over meat. Cover and simmer for 1 1/2 to 2 hours, turning occasionally.

# BARBECUED
## BEAR STEAK

| | |
|---|---|
| 2 lbs. bear steak, cut into 2 inch cubes | 1 onion, sliced |
| 1 slice salt pork, cut up | 1 tbsp. lemon juice |
| 1 cup catsup | 1 tsp. salt |
| 1/3 cup steak sauce | 1 tbsp. chili powder |
| 2 tbsp. vinegar | 3 tbsp. butter or margarine |

Trim all fat from bear steak and cut into 2 inch cubes. Put margarine or butter in a heavy frying pan, sear meat on all sides along with salt pork. Place meat in a casserole dish.

Add the rest of the ingredients to frying pan and bring to a boil, stirring constantly. Pour sauce over meat in casserole.

Cover and bake at 325 F until tender, approximately 2 hours.

# CHAPTER TWO · SMALL GAME

Notes:

Dress all game as soon as possible to ensure freshness and the prevention of bacterial growth.

If the intestines have been shot up, and this material has gotten onto the flesh, it must be carefully cut and wiped away.

Look for any yellowish fatty kernels under each front shoulder and the small of the back. If these are not removed there will be an unpleasant taste.

Old and tough animals may require parboiling for tenderness.

# RABBITS AND HARES

Although there are different types of rabbits and hares, they all have certain things in common. Certain traits such as long ears, long powerful hind legs and great speed are common to all rabbits and hares. Most are grayish to brown on top and white underneath. The common snowshoe rabbit changes to white all over during the winter months. Depending on the type of animal, the weight varies from 2 - 8 lbs.

All rabbits and hares are vegetarians and can be found in every locale of North America.

Rabbits and hares are an excellent table meat as can be seen by the number of domestic rabbit breeders found today.

✳

## WESTERN SPICY

## RABBIT

| | |
|---|---|
| 1 medium rabbit | 2 tbsp. oil |
| 1 onion, chopped | 2 quarts water |
| 1 cup vinegar | 3 tsp. red chili powder |
| 1 tsp. salt | 1/2 cup cornmeal |

Cut rabbit into serving pieces, place in large saucepan and brown in oil.  Add remaining ingredients and simmer for 1 1/2 hours or until meat is tender.  Add cornmeal gradually to pan, blending thoroughly.  Simmer 10 minutes until the sauce thickens.

## STEWED WILD RABBIT

| | |
|---|---|
| 5 lbs. wild rabbit | 1/4 tsp. pepper |
| 1 1/2 cups flour | 3/4 cup oil |
| 2 quarts water | 12 boiling onions |
| 8 carrots, sliced | 2 tsp. salt |

### DUMPLINGS

| | |
|---|---|
| 2 cups flour | 1 tbsp. baking powder |
| 1/2 tsp. salt | 1 tbsp. oil |
| 1 cup milk | |

Cut rabbit into serving pieces, sprinkle with pepper. Dredge in flour and brown in oil. Drain off oil, add water and salt, simmer, covered, for 2 hours. Add vegetables, simmer 1 hour.

Combine dry ingredients for dumplings add oil and milk and stir. Drop dumplings into boiling stew water, cover and cook 10 to 12 minutes.

※

# RABBIT DELIGHT

| | |
|---|---|
| *1 young rabbit* | *1/2 cup mushrooms, chopped* |
| *1 tbsp. fat* | *1 tbsp. parsley, chopped* |
| *1 cup broth or water with 1 chicken* | *pinch of ginger* |
| *bouillon cube* | *1/2 tsp. salt* |
| *1/4 cup lemon juice* | *1/4 tsp. pepper* |
| *3/4 cup orange juice* | *2 green peppers, chopped* |

Cut up the rabbit and brown pieces in fat in a heavy pot. Add broth and other ingredients, season with salt, pepper and ginger. Cover and cook slowly until tender.

# RABBIT

## ·N·

## GRAVY

| | |
|---|---|
| 1 1/2 cups cider vinegar | 2 rabbits, cut into serving pieces |
| 1 onion, sliced | 1 1/2 cups all purpose flour |
| 1 tbsp. dry mustard | 1/4 tsp. ground nutmeg |
| 2 tsp. salt | 1 tsp. sugar |
| 1/2 tsp. pepper | clear bacon fat |

Combine onion, mustard, vinegar, salt and pepper.  Drop in rabbit pieces, covering pieces completely.  Let stand for 1 hour, turning rabbit occasionally.

Mix 1 cup of flour with nutmeg and sugar in a paper bag.  Drain rabbit pieces then put a few pieces at a time in the bag and shake well. Put enough bacon fat in a skillet to brown rabbit pieces.

When all have been browned, remove meat and pour off all but 1/2 cup fat.  Stir in 1/2 cup of flour.  Gradually stir in 3 cups of boiling water.  Simmer, stirring constantly till thickened.  Arrange rabbit pieces in gravy; cover and simmer for 1 1/2 to 2 hours.

✳

# RABBIT HOT POT
## CASSEROLE

*1 wild rabbit, dressed*
*4 carrots, peeled and sliced*
*4 potatoes, peeled and sliced*
*1 package onion soup mix*
*2 1/2 cups hot water*

Cut rabbit into serving pieces and wash well. Blanch rabbit by putting it into a saucepan. Cover with water and bring to a boil. Remove rabbit from the saucepan and place in a greased casserole dish. Cover rabbit with the carrots and potatoes. Mix soup with the hot water and pour over vegetables. Cover and bake at 350 F for 2 hours.

✳

# POT ROAST OF RABBIT

*rabbit, cut into serving pieces*          *milk*
*flour*                                              *oil*

Dip rabbit in milk then coat with flour. Fry in hot oil until browned.

*SAUCE:*

*2 tbsp. melted butter*          *pinch of thyme*
*2 onion, chopped*               *3 1/2 cups tomato juice*
*1 clove garlic, crushed*        *1 tsp. worcestershire sauce*
*1 tbsp. parsley flakes*         *salt and pepper*

Mix together all ingredients for sauce and pour over rabbit. Simmer covered for 1 1/2 hours.

# STEWED
# RABBIT

| | |
|---|---|
| 1 rabbit, cut in serving pieces | 4 cups stewed tomatoes |
| 1/2 lb. bacon, chopped | 1/4 cup tomato paste |
| 3 tbsp. cooking oil | 1/4 tsp. red pepper |
| 1 clove garlic, crushed | 1/2 tsp. oregano |
| 1 cup onion, finely chopped | 4 tbsp. margarine |
| 6 bay leaves | 1 tbsp. parsley |
| 1/4 tsp. pepper | 1/2 cup dry red wine |
| 1/2 tsp. salt | flour |

Heat oil over medium heat in a deep saucepan. Add bacon and bay leaves to hot oil. Add onions and saute till golden brown. Add crushed garlic clove and pepper to pot and cook until mixture has well browned. Add tomato paste, stewed tomatoes, red pepper, oregano, margarine, parsley and salt.

Bring mixture to a boil, remove from heat. Dredge rabbit sections with flour and brown in a hot skillet. When meat is brown, add red wine. Simmer for 5 minutes, then add rabbit and wine to the saucepan. Simmer rabbit and sauce for 20 minutes.

Serve with rice or noodles.

✳

# BAKED STUFFED

# RABBIT

*1 rabbit*
*2 large carrots, quartered*
*4 strips of bacon or salt pork*
*1 to 2 cups hot water*

*STUFFING:*

*2 cups mashed poatoes*
*1 tbsp. butter*
*pinch of salt*
*pinch of pepper*
*pinch of savory*
*2 stalks of celery, chopped*

Skin and clean rabbit, wash with warm salted water.  Mix stuffing ingredients and fill body of rabbit with this stuffing and sew it up.

Place rabbit breast down on rack of baking pan, with legs folded under the body and fastened in this position.  Place quartered carrots beside it on the rack. Fasten strips of bacon or pork over back of rabbit with toothpicks to keep the flesh from drying out.

Place pan in a 400 F oven for 10 minutes; then pour on a cup or two of hot water over meat and continue cooking until tender, about 1 hour. Remove bacon for the last 10 minutes and let the rabbit brown.

# CURRIED
# RABBIT

2 onions, chopped

1 rabbit, cut into serving pieces

flour

3 tbsp. bacon drippings

1 tbsp. curry powder

dash cayenne

3 tbsp. warm water

1 cup of stock

2 apples, peeled and sliced

Dredge meat pieces with flour and brown in bacon drippings. Remove pieces of rabbit and put back in pan with sauteed onions. In a cup, mix together curry powder, cayenne and warm water to make a paste.

Spread paste over pieces of rabbit and put back in pan with sauteed onions. Pour over stock, stir and cover. Simmer for 20 minutes. Add apple slices and continue to simmer for 15 minutes.

# RABBIT - HAM
# CROQUETTES

| | |
|---|---|
| 2 tbsp. butter or margarine | 2/3 cup ground cooked ham |
| 2 1/2 tbsp. flour | 1 tsp. chopped parsley |
| dash of dry mustard | 1 tsp. chopped green pepper |
| 3/4 cup milk | 1 egg, beaten |
| 1 tsp. onion juice or grated onion | 3 cups fine dry bread crumbs |

1 1/3 cups chopped cooked rabbit meat

Melt butter or margarine and stir in flour and mustard. Cook until mixture bubbles. Add milk gradually, stirring constantly. Add onion and cook over low heat until sauce is thick and smooth, stirring occasionally. Add rabbit, ham, parsley and green pepper. Cool. If mixture is very soft, chill it until it is firm enough to handle easily. Shape into eight croquettes. Dip them in the beaten egg, then roll them in bread crumbs.

Fry croquettes in deep fat, 360 F, for about 4 minutes, or until golden brown.

✳

## PARMESAN RABBIT

1 rabbit
1/2 cup bread crumbs
1/2 cup parmesan cheese

salt and pepper
1/4 lb. butter
1/2 cup tomato juice

1 egg

Cut rabbit into generous serving pieces. Flatten by pounding meat gently. In a bowl, mix bread crumbs and parmesan cheese together. In another bowl, beat an egg with salt and pepper.

Roll pieces of meat in crumbs, then in the beaten egg and then again in crumb mixture. Fry in butter over medium heat for 30 minutes. Add tomato juice and cook for another hour over very low heat.

✳

## CRABAPPLE RABBIT ROAST

1 pint crabapples
1 rabbit, dressed
1 lemon, halved
1 clove garlic
1 tsp. salt

1 tsp. pepper
1 1/2 tsp. summer savory
2 tbsp. crabapple jelly
2 strips bacon
1 tbsp. parsley

Wash and pat dry rabbit. Rub inside and outside of rabbit well with lemon halves. Then rub well with garlic clove. Sprinkle cavity with salt, pepper and savory. Coat breast with crabapple jelly and cover with bacon strips. Place rabbit in a small roasting pan: cover and bake at 350 F for 1 1/2 hours.

To serve, garnish with parsley and whole preserved crabapples.

# RABBIT STEW
# AND SLAP JACKS

| | |
|---|---|
| 1 wild rabbit | 4 carrots, sliced |
| 1 tsp. salt | 2 cups turnip, diced |
| 1/2 tsp. pepper | 4 potatoes, diced |
| 1 medium onion, chopped | 2 tbsp. flour or cornstarch |

Parboil rabbit for 40 minutes and drain. Cover with water; add salt and pepper, then bring to a boil. Add vegetables and cook for 1 hour. Thicken with flour or cornstarch. Add more water when necessary.

## SLAP JACKS:

| | |
|---|---|
| 3/4 cup water | 1/4 tsp. pepper |
| 2 cups flour | 1/4 tsp. sage |

1/2 tsp. salt

Combine all ingredients except water. Make a well; then add water, stirring as you pour. Turn out onto a floured board and knead a few times. Roll out to 1/2 inch thickness and cut into squares. Add to boiling stew and cover. Cook for 15 to 20 minutes.

## ROAST RABBIT

oil or fat                          2 cups dried bread crumbs
1 rabbit, dressed                   1 tbsp. onion, diced
salt and pepper                     1 tbsp. parsley
                1/2 lb. sausage meat

Combine bread crumbs, sausage meat, parsley and onions. Wash rabbit and pat dry. Stuff cavity with bread crumb mixture and sew it closed. Add 1 cup of water and roast uncovered at 325 F for 1 1/2 to 2 hours.

✳

## SWEET AND SOUR RABBIT

2 to 3 lbs. rabbit, cut-up          1 cup pineapple chunks
1/4 cup margarine                   1 medium green pepper
1 1/2 tsp. salt                     1 1/2 tsp. cornstarch
1/4 tsp. pepper                     1/4 cup sugar
1 cup pineapple juice               1/2 cup water
                1/2 cup vinegar

Heat margarine in a skillet and brown rabbit pieces over medium heat. Sprinkle on salt and pepper. Add pineapple juice and vinegar. Cover and simmer for 45 minutes or until meat is tender.

Mix in pineapple chunks and green pepper. Simmer for 5 minutes. Mix sugar and cornstarch into the water. Stir into the rabbit mixture. Simmer for 5 minutes. Serve.

# RABBIT
## SOUP

leftover rabbit meat and bones      1/4 tsp. thyme
1 soup bone      1 bay leaf
1/4 lb. salt pork      4 cups chicken broth
3 carrots, sliced      1 cup potatoes, diced
1 onion, quartered      1/2 cup celery, diced
1 clove garlic      1/2 cup carrots, diced
1/4 tsp. parsley      salt and pepper

Remove all meat from rabbit bones and set aside. In a kettle, combine bones and soup bones and salt pork. Add carrots, onion, garlic, parsley, thyme and bay leaf.

Cover with water and simmer until almost dry. Add chicken broth and simmer 15 minutes. Strain broth and adjust the seasoning to taste. Add potatoes and simmer until tender.

Add celery and carrots and cook 20 minutes longer. Add rabbit meat.

Heat thoroughly and serve.

# BEAVER

The beaver is a small game animal with a heavy body, short legs, large webbed feet and scaly tail. The fur is dense and varies from reddish chestnut to deep brown and almost black.

The average weight of a mature beaver is 40 - 50 lbs. In order to survive, it lives on tree bark, grasses, and aquatic plants.

The beaver is an aquatic animal which, if necessary, creates its own water reservoir by use of dams. They build houses out of sticks and mud, with water entrances; but tall enough to be above the water line. They are tireless workers and very docile. When alarmed, they slap their tail on the water as a warning. The major enemy of the beaver is man, but they sometimes fall prey to the larger predators such as the wolf.

Beaver is an excellent table meat. Everyone should try beaver tails before they die.

✳

## BEAVER WITH STUFFING

Parboil 2 hind beaver quarters for 30 minutes and rinse. Repeat method twice. Make stuffing of your choice. In a roasting pan lay one hind quarter and cover with stuffing. Put remaining hind quarter on top and tie two together with string. Pour on 2 cups of water; cover and roast for 35 to 40 minutes, at 325 F.

NOTE: To determine parboiling time, the beaver will be ready to put in the oven when it can be pierced easily.

## ROAST BEAVER

1 beaver, quartered
2 tbsp. pickling spice
2 tbsp. dry mustard
1/2 cup dry wine

1/2 cup brown sugar
1 cup pineapple juice
1 tsp. lemon juice
1/2 cup water

Parboil beaver quarters for 30 minutes and rinse. Repeat method twice. Place beaver quarters in a clean pot with enough water to cover; add pickling spice and boil for 20 minutes. Drain and rinse with warm water. Place meat in a roast pan. Combine dry mustard, dry wine, brown sugar, pineapple juice, lemon juice and water. Pour over meat and roast for 1 hour at 325 F, basting often.

## BOILED BEAVER

Hind quarter of beaver
1 large onion
3 carrots, sliced
2 tsp. salt
water

Boil beaver for 1/2 hours. Drain and rinse. Repeat method twice. Cover with water again then add remaining ingredients. Cover and boil until tender. Dispose of vegetables as they will hold most of the wild taste from the beaver.

## BEAVER TAILS

## IN SAUCE

2 beaver tails
1/2 cup white vinegar
1 tsp. salt
2 tsp. baking soda
1/4 cup flour
1/2 tsp. salt
1/4 tsp. pepper

1/4 cup oil
1/4 cup cider vinegar
1 tsp. dry mustard
1 tsp. sugar
1/2 tsp. garlic powder
2 tbsp. worcestershire sauce

The day before, skin the beaver tails. Cover tails in cold water and wash thoroughly. Rinse. Place tails in a pot and cover with cold water. Add 1/2 cup of white vinegar and 1 teaspoon of salt. Soak overnight. Drain.

Place tails in a heavy pot. Cover with water and add 2 teaspoons of baking soda. Cover and bring to a boil. Reduce heat and simmer for 12 to 15 minutes. Drain.

Combine flour, salt and pepper. Dredge beaver tails in the seasoned flour. Heat the oil in a skillet. Add beaver tails and saute over low heat until tender.

Combine vinegar, mustard, sugar, garlic powder and worcestershire sauce. Add to the skillet and simmer covered for 20 minutes, basting often.

# GROUNDHOG, WOODCHUCK

The groundhog, also known as the woodchuck, is a small animal, weighing from 5-10 lbs. and generally has coarse brown fur. The groundhog lives in a burrow of his own making. This house has several tunnels and several emergency exits. Usually you will find three sleeping chambers at the end of the tunnel. Because of its low intelligence level, it is easily killed by man. The groundhog is known to be 90% vegetarian.

Groundhog is an excellent table meat that is easily found throughout the countryside in open grassy areas and farmer's fields. The hide, when tanned, is extremely durable.

## COOKED GROUNDHOG

*1 carrot, sliced*  
*2 onions, sliced*  
*2 potatoes, sliced*  

*1 tsp. garlic*  
*1 groundhog*  
*water*  

To clean a ground hog, you first must remove the insides. Make a fire outside and scorch hair from the ground hog. Use a sharp knife to scrape all scorched hair off. Wash and clean groundhog with cold water. Put in a large pot with enough water to cover and add all remaining ingredients. Boil until meat is tender, then dispose of vegetables. Refrigerate meat until the next day when it will be best for eating. Can be reheated.

※

# PRESSURE COOKED
# GROUNDHOG

*1 groundhog, dressed*
*salt*
*flour*
*bacon fat*

NOTE:  Be sure to remove the kernel from behind the front legs to keep from spoling the flavor of the meat.

Cut the groundhog into serving pieces and roll in flour.  Sprinkle with salt; slightly brown the meat in bacon fat.  Put the insert pan in pressure cooker with 1/2 inch of water on the bottom.  Put in the meat pieces and cook for about 70 minutes with 15 pound pressure.

✳

## ROAST GROUNDHOG

| | |
|---|---|
| 1 groundhog, dressed | 1/4 cup lemon juice |
| 3 cups bread crumbs | 1/2 cup evaporated milk |
| 1 small onion, chopped fine | 4 tsp. bacon fat |
| salt and pepper to taste | 1 cup cooking oil |

Combine oil and lemon juice and marinate groundhog in this overnight. Mix together bread crumbs, onion, salt and pepper. Mix in milk until well combined. Remove meat from the marinade and pat dry. Stuff bread crumb mixture into the groundhog and sew cavity closed. Brush with bacon fat and place in a roasting pan. Cover and roast at 300 F. for 1 1/2 to 2 hours. You may need to add a little water.

✳

## FRIED WOODCHUCK

| | |
|---|---|
| 1 woodchuck | 4 tbsp. fat |
| 1 tbsp. salt | 1/2 tsp. salt |
| 1 cup flour | 1/4 tsp. pepper |

Skin and clean woodchuck and cut into 6 or 7 pieces. Put in pot, add salt and enough water to cover, and parboil for 1 hour.

Remove meat from the broth, and drain. Dredge meat in flour, salt and pepper. Melt fat in heavy skillet and saute woodchuck until nicely browned.

✳

# MUSKRAT

The muskrat is a small animal which weighs approximately 2 lbs. They are dark brown in color and light grey or tan through the belly. They adapt well to aquatic life because of their scaly flattened tail, and valves or flaps which prevent water entering their nose, mouth, and ears.

Muskrat prefer to live in fresh water marshes and slow moving streams. They are known to have several houses for dwelling and feeding. The food source for muskrat consists of cattails, bullrushes, submerged pond weed, crayfish and frogs.

Similar to the beaver, they are active throughout the year. Many people consider muskrat a delicacy and look forward to the trapping season when the meat is utilized as well as the hide.

✳

# BAKED MUSKRAT

*2 muskrat, skinned and cleaned*
*1/2 cup flour*
*1/4 tsp. sage*
*1/4 cup lemon juice*

*1/4 cup water*
*1/2 tsp. salt*
*1/4 tsp. pepper*
*bacon strips to cover (optional)*

Boil meat for about 30 minutes; drain and rinse. Repeat. Mix flour, salt, pepper and sage. Rub the mixture thoroughly into the meat, making sure it is well floured. Place meat into a roast pan, adding lemon juice and water. (If using bacon strips, cover meat entirely). Bake at 325 F until tender.

## FRIED MUSKRAT

| | |
|---|---|
| 2 muskrat, cut into serving piece | 1/4 cup water |
| 1/2 tsp. poultry seasoning | 2 tbsp. onion, finely chopped |
| 1/2 tsp. salt | 2 tbsp. celery, finely chopped |
| 1/4 tsp. pepper | bacon fat, margarine or butter |
| 1/4 tsp. sage | 1/2 cup water |

Mix flour, salt, pepper and poultry seasoning. rub thoroughly into serving pieces, making sure pieces are thoroughly coated. Fry in butter, margarine or bacon fat. Add 1/2 cup of water to frying pan and cook slowly for about five minutes. Add celery and onions.

Stir and cook for 1/2 hour or until done.

✳

## MUSKRAT HASH

| | |
|---|---|
| 1 cup barbecue sauce | 1 tsp. poultry seasoning |
| 3 muskrats | 1 tsp. sage |
| 2 tsp. salt | 2 large onions, diced |
| 1 tsp. pepper | 4 tbsp. margarine |
| 1 tsp. garlic salt | |

Boil muskrat until well cooked, approximately 2 1/2 hours. Drain. Rinse and remove bones. Combine onions, spices and barbecue sauce to meat. Place meat mixture into a lightly greased casserole dish. Pour melted margarine over the top.

Cover and bake at 300 F for 1 hour.

# MUSKRAT LOAF

2 lbs. muskrat meat, cooked,
   chopped, bones removed
2 eggs, slightly beaten
1/2 cup bread crumbs
1 cup milk

1/4 tsp. thyme
1 1/2 tsp. salt
1/2 tsp. pepper
1/2 cup catsup
2 tbsp. margarine

1 medium onion, chopped fine
1/4 tsp. sage

Place muskrat in a large bowl and mix in remaining ingredients.
Pack lightly into a greased loaf pan and roast in a 350 F oven for 30 to 35
minutes.

# PORCUPINE

The porcupine is recognized by its heavy dark brown or blackish body and a heavy short tail. The hair on the porcupine hides the quills unless the creature is alarmed.

The porcupine usually weighs 8 - 15 lbs., and is known to be very clumsy and slow moving. Their diet consists of most plants, nuts, and tree bark.

Although the porcupine is well protected, it does have its enemies. Usually the porcupine wins, but on occasion, an animal learns to flip the porcupine and is able to attack the defenceless belly. Contrary to many beliefs, the porcupine does not shoot its quills.

When properly prepared, the meat is very good.

✳

# BARBECUE PORCUPINE

*1/2 porcupine to each serving*
*barbecue sauce*

Soak meat overnight in vinegar and water. Roast on broiler pan (rack at center of oven) at 350 F for 1 hour. Spread barbecue sauce over meat and cook for 10 minutes. Turn meat over and spread barbecue sauce on meat and cook for an additional 10 minutes.

# APPLE-ROASTED
# PORCUPINE

| | |
|---|---|
| 1 porcupine, dressed | salt and pepper to taste |
| 3 apples, unreeled, quartered | 2 tbsp. sugar |
| and seeds removed | 4 cups water |

Parboil porcupine for 1 hour in salted water to cover. Drain and rinse. Place meat in a roast pan. Add apples and sprinkle the apples with 2 tablespoons of sugar. Add water. Sprinkle meat with salt and pepper. Cover and roast 30 to 40 minutes at 375 F.

# RACCOON

The raccoon is a nocturnal animal with good vision and hearing. The naked soles of their feet are extremely sensitive to touch, and the coat of the raccoon ranges from black to tawny, pale grey and blonde. They have prominent black rings on their tails and their nickname "Bandit" bespeaks their famous black facial mask over their cheeks, eyes and nose. The average raccoon weighs about 17 lbs.

Raccoons prefer forested areas near water, river valleys and farmland. They usually live in hollow trees, logs, caves, mines and other animal's burrows.

Raccoons are omnivorous, eating young birds, small mammals, carrion, poultry, fish, frogs, eggs, fruit, nuts, berries, grain and corn.

Although raccoons do not hibernate, they are inactive and stay in their dens when the temperature is below 26 F.

Raccoons are also considered an excellent table meat.

## OLD FASHIONED
## COOKED RACCOON

1 raccoon, dressed                    sage
1 tbsp. salt                          salt and pepper to taste
          1 tsp. baking soda
          water

Cut raccoon into serving pieces and soak in salted water and baking soda overnight. Drain and rinse. Place meat pieces in a baking dish and add 2 cups of water. Sprinkle with sage, salt and pepper. Cover with aluminum foil and bake at 375 F until tender.

※

## RACCOON ROAST

1 raccoon, dressed              2 celery stalks, chopped
2 chicken bouillon cubes        salt and pepper to taste
3 onions, sliced thin           1 cup water

In a large pot, parboil meat for about 45 minutes in salt water (1 tablespoon of salt per quart). This helps tenderize the meat. Rinse well.
Transfer raccoon to roasting pan. Add celery, onions, chicken cubes, salt and pepper. Add water. Cover and bake at 325 F about 1 1/2 to 2 hours or until tender.

# RACCOON AND DRESSING

1 raccoon, dressed                         1/2 tsp. salt
salt                                       1 tsp. sage
2 cups potatoes, mashed                    1/2 tsp. poultry seasoning
1 onion, chopped                           pepper to taste
2 cups bread crumbs                        1/4 cup bacon dripping

minutes.  Drain and rinse.  Combine remaining ingredients in a
large bowl.  Add a little water if too dry.  Place raccoon pieces on 1/2 of
the shallow baking dish.  Dot with margarine and sprinkle with salt and
pepper.  Spread the dressing on remaining half of the baking dish cover
with aluminum foil..  Bake at 350 F for 60 to 90 minutes.

# RACCOON DELIGHT

1 raccoon, dressed                         1 large onion, chopped
salt and pepper                            1 large apple, peeled and diced
2 cups vegetables, cut-up                  1 (28 oz.) can sauerkraut
2 sweet potatoes, peeled and diced   a few drops of tabasco sauce

Salt and pepper the entire carcass.  Combine vegetables, potatoes, onion and apples.  Stuff cavity of the raccoon.  Place in a roasting
pan stomach side up.  Drain sauerkraut, reserve the juice and spread
sauerkraut over the vegetables in cavity. Mix a few drops of tabasco sauce
with reserved juice and pour over the raccoon. Cover and roast at 350 F
for 3 to 4 hours or until very tender.

# SQUIRREL

Squirrels today are a more common sight in the cities and towns than they are in their natural woodland habitat.

Nuts and seed are the main stay of the squirrel's diet. They are busy gatherers, and store their catch for winter use.

Squirrels are found in almost all of the temperate zones. They are grey to black in color with long bushy tails, and weigh only 1 - 1 1/2 lbs.

The meat of the squirrel is considered by many to be a delectable dish.

✳

# BROILED SQUIRREL

*2 squirrels*
*1 tsp. salt*
*dash of pepper*
*4 tbsp. melted butter for basting*

Skin and clean squirrels. Wash thoroughly and pat dry. Cut in half lengthwise and rub with salt and pepper. Place halves on broiling rack and brush with fat. Broil 5 inches from source of heat, 20 minutes on each side. Baste every few minutes with melted butter and dripping.

# SQUIRREL FRICASSEE

| | |
|---|---|
| 1 squirrel | 4 slices bacon, cut up |
| 1/2 tsp. salt | 1 tbsp. diced onion |
| dash of pepper | 1 1/2 tsp. lemon juice |
| 1/2 cup flour | 1/3 cup broth |

Skin and clean squirrel, being sure to remove scent glands from forelegs. Wash thoroughly and cut squirrel into serving pieces. Rub pieces with salt and pepper, then dredge with flour. Cut up bacon and cook over low heat until crisp. Add the squirrel and pan fry with the bacon for 20 minutes, until nicely browned. Add diced onion, lemon juice and broth. Cover tightly and simmer for 2 hours.

# SNAPPING TURTLE

The snapping turtle is a reptile having a large head with a strongly hooked beak. With an exceedingly rough shell and very long tail, it is easy for them to protect themselves by hiding within their shell. Snapping turtles are brown in color and range in size from 8 - 20 inches in length.

Snapping turtles are found in most bodies of fresh water. Their diet includes aquatic invertebrates, fish, reptiles, birds, mammals, carrion, and vegetation. Underwater, they are inoffensive but on land they will strike out. The snapping turtle is found from Canada in the north, south to Mexico and west to the Rockies. The meat is considered a delicacy by many. Properly prepared, it is succulent and has a unique taste.

# TURTLE
# WITH MUSHROOMS

*2 cups turtle meat, cooked*
*1 cup mushrooms, stems and pieces*
*2 cups white sauce*
*1 tbsp. sherry*

(See "Sauces .." chapter for a variety of white sauce recipes.)

Combine all ingredients in a saucepan and heat slowly. Serve over toast.

✳

# TURTLE CHOWDER

*1 lb. cubed turtle meat*           *1 cup green peppers, chopped*
*1 cup celery, chopped*                          *2 tsp. salt*
*1 cup peas*                            *1 medium onion, chopped*
*1 cup carrots, sliced*                          *1/2 cup milk*
*1 cup turnip, sliced*                  *2 tbsp. flour or cornstarch*

Boil meat in salted water until done, about 1 hour. Then add all vegetables and cook over medium heat until tender. Remove from heat and add milk. Thicken with flour or cornstarch.

# TURTLE RAGOUT

1 onion, chopped

2 tbsp. butter or margarine

1 tbsp. flour

1 bay leaf

1 clove garlic

1 cup water

2 lbs. turtle meat, diced

1/4 cup sherry

Saute onion in butter or margarine until tender. Blend in flour. Add remaining ingredients and simmer for 30 minutes.

✳

# TURTLE SOUP

4 potatoes, quartered

4 carrots, quartered

1 cup celery, chopped

1 cup peas

1 onion, diced

1 cup turnip, quartered

1 lb. turtle meat, cubed

1 tbsp. sugar (optional)

flour to thicken

1 cup milk

Boil meat until nearly tender. Add all vegetables and simmer; covered for 1 hour. Add 1 cup of milk and thicken with flour. Mix in sugar, if desired.

✳

# WILD OMELETTE

*1 tbsp. fat*
*salt and pepper*
*6 eggs*
*1/2 cup leftover turtle or other wild meat, chopped*
*1/4 cup milk*                                         *cheese, grated*
*1/2 cup onions, chopped*

Combine eggs, milk, onions, and seasonings (salt and pepper). Heat fat in a skillet. Add mixture with a spatula; allow liquid to run underneath. Spread chopped meat and cheese over the eggs, then fold. When the cheese has melted, serve with toast.

# BULLFROG

The bullfrog is the largest frog, measuring 3 1/2 - 6 inches. It is a plain or nearly green color with a netlike pattern of gray or brown on a green background. It is whitish, often mottled with gray, with a yellowish throat underneath. They have long hind legs, and are narrow waisted and smooth skinned.

They are aquatic amphibians living in lakes, ponds, bogs or sluggish portions of streams.

The legs of the bullfrog are considered a delicacy throughout many parts of North America as well as Europe.

# FROG LEGS

The hind legs of the frog are the only part that can be eaten. Cut legs from body, wash in cold water, turn skin down and strip off. Cover with cold water, drain, dry and use as desired.

## FRIED FROG LEGS

Season prepared legs with salt and pepper, dip into fine cracker crumbs, then into slightly beaten egg and again into crumbs. Let stand for 15 to 20 minutes. Fry in hot fat, until browned.

## SAUTEED FROG LEGS

Prepare frog legs as above and brown in skillet in a small amount of hot fat.

## BREADED FROG LEGS

6 - 7 pairs frogs' legs, cleaned
1/2 tsp. salt
1/4 tsp. pepper

1 tbsp. onion, grated
1 tsp. lemon juice
flour for dredging
small amount of butter for frying

Mix salt and pepper with enough flour to dredge the frogs' legs. Saute onion in butter. Add frogs' legs and lemon juice. Cook, covered over low heat ( or low flame) for 10 to 15 minutes until legs are brown and tender.

## DEEP FRIED
## FROG LEGS

25 frog legs
1 cup flour
1/2 tsp. salt

1/4 tsp. pepper
3 eggs beaten
2 1/2 cups

bread crumbs

Wash and dry frog legs. In a paper bag; put flour, salt and pepper. Add legs to bag and shake; then dip into beaten eggs. Roll in bread crumbs and deep fry.

## CREAM SAUCE
## FROG LEGS

2 lbs. frog legs
1/3 cup flour
1 1/2 tsp. salt
1/2 tsp. dried tarragon

1/4 cup butter or margarine
2 tbsp. finely chopped onion
1 1/2 cups light cream
2 tbsp. parsley

1/4 tsp. pepper

Separate frog legs into individual legs. In bag, combine flour, salt, tarragon and pepper. Shake frog legs in flour mixture a few at a time to coat thoroughly. Reserve 1 tablespoon of flour mixture.

In a large skillet brown frog legs in butter. Cook covered until tender, about 25 minutes. Remove legs, and keep warm.

In same skillet cook onions, until tender, but not brown. Blend in reserved flour mixture. Stir in light cream; cook and stir until thickened. Spoon over frog legs. Garnish with parsley.

✳

## BATTER-FRIED
## FROG LEGS

| | |
|---|---|
| *1 egg, beaten* | *1/2 cup corn meal* |
| *1/2 tsp. salt* | *1/8 tsp. pepper* |
| *2 lbs. frog legs* | *1/2 cup oil* |

Mix egg, corn meal, salt and pepper to form a batter. Dip frog legs in batter, fry in oil in heavy skillet for 25 minutes turning so they brown evenly on all sides.

# CHAPTER THREE · GAME BIRDS·

The age of the bird is an important consideration in selecting the recipe to be used. The older the bird, the longer it must be cooked. Older birds are usually used in soups and stews.

A young pheasant has a pliable spur. The breastbone of a young partridge will break easily, and the leg will be plump near the foot.

The claws of a young bird are sharp; those of an old one are blunt.

If stuffing the bird before cooking, always use a cool stuffing, because bacteria will start working and render your bird unpalatable, if not unsafe to eat.

## DUCKS

Ducks can generally be divided into two groups. The first one being those ducks which take their food on or from the surface of the water **(puddle ducks)** and those taking their food from under the surface **(diving ducks)**. Puddle ducks (mallards, pintails, wood ducks and black ducks - for example) have broad flat bills with a turned down projection at the tip. The legs are placed near the center of the body making them adequate swimmers and well balanced walkers. Diving ducks (bluebills, redheads, ruddy ducks) eat more animal food than puddle ducks, in addition to vegetable matter. The legs are placed near the rear of the body making them excellent swimmers but clumsy on land.

All ducks require open water and are therefore migratory in northern North America.

Ducks are extremely common throughout the United States and Canada and provide excellent eating. Usually the surface feeding puddle ducks provide the more palatable fare.

# 101.
# ROAST DUCK WITH
# WILD RICE CASSEROLE

*2 strips bacon*
*2 wild ducks, dressed*
*1 celery stalk, cut in half*
*2 small onions*
*2 cups water*

Wash ducks in cold water and pat dry. Put half piece of celery and one onion in every duck cavity. Place ducks in a roasting pan, breast side up. Pour in cold water and place bacon strips over ducks. Cover and bake at 350 F. until meat is tender about 1 1/2 hours. Remove bacon strips and brown ducks. Remove ducks from pan and keep in a warm place.

## WILD RICE CASSEROLE

*1 tomato, peeled and chopped*       *1/4 cup mushrooms*
*1/4 lb. wild rice*                  *salt and pepper*
*1/2 cup bacon, diced*               *1 tsp. garlic powder*
*1/4 cup green onions, sliced*       *parmesan cheese*

Wash rice in cold water. Drain. Put rice into a saucepan, cover with water and bring to a boil. Reduce heat and simmer for 60 minutes. Drain. Saute bacon, green onions and mushrooms for 5 minutes.

Put rice in a casserole dish and stir in tomatoes, garlic powder and bacon mixture. Season with salt and pepper. Sprinkle cheese over the casserole and bake for 20 minutes at 300 F. Serve with the ducks.

# 102.
# BLUEBERRY
## DUCK ROAST

1 1/2 cup blueberries
2 tbsp. vinegar, white
2 tsp. brown sugar
1 tsp. salt
1/2 tsp. pepper

1/4 tsp. ground cloves
1/4 tsp. nutmeg
1 tbsp. vegetable oil
4 to 6 wild duck breasts

Combine all of ingredients except duck breasts in a blender. Process to a coarse puree. Remove bones from duck breasts, leaving skin intact. Place breasts on a rack in roaster and coat each one with blueberry mixture. Bake at 375 F for 30 minutes, basting often.

✳

## DELICIOUS ROAST DUCK

3 wild ducks
3 tsp. soya sauce
1/2 cup marmalade
1/2 tsp. salt

1/2 tsp. pepper
3 bacon strips
3 small onions
garlic powder

Place ducks in roasting pan, putting one onion inside each duck along with one teaspoon of soya sauce. Sprinkle salt, pepper and garlic powder over ducks. Then brush ducks with marmalade and sprinkle lightly with brown sugar. On each duck place one strip of bacon. Cover and place in oven at 375 F. for 60 minutes or until tender.

## DUCK IN DARK SAUCE

| | |
|---|---|
| 1 wild duck | 2 tsp. garlic salt |
| 1/2 cup cider vinegar | 1 tsp. ginger |
| 4 tbsp. white sugar | 1/4 cup soya sauce |

Wash and pat dry duck and then cut in half. Lay halves in a shallow baking pan. Mix vinegar, soya sauce, sugar and seasonings together. Put over the duck and bake, covered, at 350 F for 1 hour.

❋

## WILD DUCK SOUP

| | |
|---|---|
| duck bone scraps | 1 stalk celery and leaves, chopped |
| 1 large onion, quartered | salt |
| 3 carrots, chopped | pepper |
| 1/4 tsp. thyme | 1 cup wild rice, cooked |
| 1/4 tsp. parsley | |

In a soup kettle combine duck scraps and bones with onion, carrots, thyme, celery and parsley. Cover with cold water and slowly bring to a boil. Simmer for 1 hour, remove bones. Add wild rice and season to taste and simmer for 1 hour.

❋

# DUCK FRICASSE

| | |
|---|---|
| 2 wild ducks | 1 cup sliced mushrooms, fresh or canned |
| 1/4 cup flour | 1/2 cup sliced green peppers |
| 1/4 cup butter | 1 cup water |
| 1 medium onion, minced | 1/4 tsp. salt |
| 1 bay leaf | 1/4 tsp. pepper |

Clean and skin ducks; wash thoroughly and cut into serving portion. Dredge portions of duck in flour and season with salt and pepper. Melt butter in a heavy frying pan, add onion and bay leaf and brown pieces of duck on all sides.

Transfer pieces of duck to a greased casserole, and saute mushrooms and green peppers in remaining fat in frying pan for 3 minutes.

Add mushrooms and green peppers to duck in the casserole, add one cup of water, cover and bake until tender in a 350 F oven.

✳

# DRESSED WILD DUCKS

2 wild ducks, dressed

STUFFING:

| | |
|---|---|
| 3 cups bread crumbs | 3 tbsp. margarine |
| 1 cooking apple, diced | 1 tsp. salt |
| 1 onion, chopped finely | 1/2 cup raisins |

Combine all stuffing ingredients in a mixing bowl. Moisten with a little water. Stuff cavity of each duck. Place in a roasting pan and add 1 1/2 cups of water. Sprinkle salt and pepper on the ducks. Cover and roast at 375 F until tender.

# CURRANT
# DUCK ROAST

2 wild ducks, cleaned and washed          1 tsp. sage
2 small onions                            1 onion, chopped
4 cups bread crumbs                       2 tsp. currant jelly
1 tsp. salt                               3 tbsp. margarine
1 tsp. pepper                             cornstarch

Put one small onion in each duck cavity and parboil for one half hour. Remove onion. Then, combine remaining ingredients and fill each duck cavity.

Place ducks in a roasting pan and pour over two cups of water. Cover and roast, basting frequently for 1 1/2 hours at 350 F. Remove ducks to a warm platter and add currant jelly to liquid. Mix in some cornstarch to thicken gravy.

In the Powhatan language of the Virginian tribes, the duck was named *"Kehanquoc"*. Many Powhatan names sound like the animals they describe.

## WILD DUCK
## IN ORANGE SAUCE

breast of 4 ducks
1/2 cup oil
2 onions, sliced thin

1/4 tsp. parsley
salt and pepper to taste
butter

Combine oil, onions, parsley, salt and pepper. Marinate the duck breasts in this mixture for 3 hours. Drain and saute in butter for 20 minutes. Arrange duck on a hot platter and pour orange sauce over it.

### ORANGE SAUCE

1 cup orange juice
1 tbsp. grated orange rind

1 tbsp. cornstarch
3 tbsp. sugar

Mix cornstarch to a paste with a little orange juice. Combine the rest of the orange juice and sugar in a saucepan. Cook until it is clear and thick. Add orange rind and pour over the duck.

## HAZELNUT
## ROAST DUCK

5 1/2 lb. duck
1/2 lb. mushrooms
1 1/2 cup Tokay grapes
1 tsp. salt

Duck giblets
4 green apples
2 cups hazelnuts
1/4 tsp. pepper

2 cups apple cider

Cover duck giblets with water in small saucepan and simmer 1/2 hour. Drain, reserving 1/2 cup cooking water. Chop giblets and add to water and remaining ingredients except cider, to make dressing. Stuff duck and place breast side up on a rack in a large roasting pan. Bake in 400 oven for 1 hour, pricking the skin and basting with apple cider every 20 minutes. Reduce oven to 350 and continue to roast 2 hours more basting every 20 minutes.

# MALLARD
## BAKE

5 cooking apples                    1 cup raisins
4 bacon strips                      salt and pepper to taste
2 mallard ducks, dressed            1 1/2 cups water

Season the ducks with salt and pepper inside and out. Quarter apples and remove cores. Place 3 apple quarters in cavity of each duck along with a handful of raisins. Place ducks in a roasting pan and add 1 1/2 cups of water. Place 2 strips of bacon over each duck and place remaining pieces of apple and raisins in the pan. Bake at 350 F until tender.

# GEESE

Geese are migratory birds travelling great distances in the spring and fall. They nest on the ground, and always near water. The species included are the Canada, Brant, and Snow. Geese mate for life and keep their young with them until the following spring. The female incubates the eggs while the male stands guard. These geese feed on roots of aquatic plants, grasses and grain. They lose their flight feathers for a time after the eggs are hatched.

Among the Cree of Northern Canada, roast goose is the meat of choice at every wedding feast. Goose hunting season is a festive time and special cooking wigwams or *mi-chu-wups* are set up for the duration.

Is there anyone who hasn't heard the honking of the geese in the spring and fall or seen the familiar V of the flocks in the sky?

Goose meat is quite delectable as dinner fare.

✳

## GOOSE GIBLET SOUP

1 tbsp. butter
2 onions, diced
Liver and giblets from 8 to 10 lb.
   goose, chopped
3 carrots, peeled, diced
1/2 cup tomatoes, peeled, chopped

1/2 lb. mushrooms, slices
1 green pepper, cored, diced
1 clove garlic, minced
salt and pepper to taste
2 cups chicken stock

Melt butter in a skillet and saute onions until tender. Add giblets, and saute ten minutes over low heat. Add remaining ingredients, cover and simmer for two hours. Add liver during the last 15 minutes. Serve with rice or biscuits.

# STUFFED
# WILD GOOSE

1 wild goose, dressed

1/2 cup salad oil

salt and pepper to taste

1/4 cup flour

1 tsp. tarragon

1/2 tsp. thyme

6 strips bacon

1 cup margarine, melted

1 cup chicken bouillon

### DRESSING:

6 large potatoes, cooked
and mashed

2 tbsp. margarine

1 large onion, chopped

2 stalks celery, chopped fine

6 slices bread, crumbled

2 eggs, beaten

1 tbsp. poultry seasoning

1 tsp. salt

1/2 tsp. pepper

Combine all the ingredients for stuffing and mix thoroughly. Place goose in a roasting pan and lightly pack stuffing into cavity. Sew the opening or skewer it closed. Rub bird well with salad oil. Combine flour, salt, pepper, tarragon, and thyme. Sprinkle mixture over the bird. Lay bacon slices over the bird.

Roast at 300 F allowing 30 minutes per pound. Baste frequently. Remove bacon slices 10 to 15 minutes before removing bird from the oven to allow breast of the bird to brown.

# WILD GOOSE WITH
# APPLE AND RAISIN STUFFING

*1 (8 to 10 lb.) wild goose, dressed*
*1 large cooking apple, chopped*

*1/2 cup lemon juice*                          *1/2 cup raisins*
*1 tsp. salt*                                  *4 cups bread crumbs*
*1/2 tsp. pepper*                              *1/2 tsp. salt*
*1/2 cup margarine*                            *1/4 tsp. pepper*
*1 onion, chopped*                             *8 slices bacon*
*1/4 cup bacon fat*

Place goose in a roasting pan. Sprinkle goose inside and out with lemon juice, salt and pepper. Melt margarine in a skillet and add onions. Cook until tender. Mix in apples, raisins, bread crumbs, salt and pepper. Set aside to cool. Pack stuffing lightly into cavity of goose. Close the opening. Rub goose with bacon fat. Place strips of bacon over goose. Cover and roast at 350 F for 30 minutes per pound. Baste frequently.

# CRANBERRY ROAST GOOSE

| | |
|---|---|
| 10-11 lb. goose | Goose giblets |
| 1 quart water | 16 oz. poultry stuffing |
| 2 cups cranberries, mashed | 1/4 lb. mushrooms |
| 1 lb. stewed prunes | 1 tsp. salt |
| 1/4 tsp. pepper | 2 cups apple cider |

Simmer goose giblets in salted water for 30 minutes or until tender, chop. Skim water off fat and save. For stuffing mix prepared stuffing mix, cranberries, sliced mushrooms, mashed prunes, giblets, water and seasonings.

Stuff goose and place breast side up on a rack in a large roasting pan and roast in a 350 oven for 4 1/2 hours.

Prick the skin from time to time and baste every 15 minutes with cider and drippings.

# OPEN FIRE WILD TURKEY

| | |
|---|---|
| | 1 turkey, dressed |
| seasoning to taste | barbecue salt |

Rub barbecue salt liberally on inside of turkey. Run stick diagonally through turkey from front of tail to breast bone. Tie tightly to stick.

Roast over low fire 3 - 4 hours turning every so often. Near end of roasting period, throw seasonings to burn on fire below for additional flavor.

# ROAST PHEASANT

2 pheasants                    3/4 cup butter
1/2 tsp. thyme                 2 tsp. salt
18 juniper berries             1/8 tsp. pepper
2 lbs. seedless grapes         1 cup broken nut meats

Melt butter and stir in seasoning and crushed juniper berries. Rub birds inside and out with butter mixture. Mash half the grapes, mix in rest of grapes and remaining ingredients. Stuff birds and truss. Place birds on rack in baking pan and bake at 425 for 15 minutes. Reduce heat to 350 and roast 45 minutes more basting every 10 minutes with drippings.

PHEASANT

# 113.

# TURKEY WITH
# OYSTER STUFFING

8 lb. turkey                          1 1/2 cup water

1 cup butter

## STUFFING

| | |
|---|---|
| 8 cups cornbread | 2 scallions, sliced |
| 10 mushrooms, chopped | 1 cup pecans, chopped |
| 18 oysters, chopped | turkey giblets |
| 1 egg | 1 clove garlic, minced |
| 2 tbsp. parsley, chopped | 1/2 tsp. savory |
| 1/4 tsp. pepper | 1 tsp. salt |
| 1/2 cup giblet water | 1/4 cup butter |

Simmer giblets in water for 20 to 30 minutes. Remove from water, cool and chop. Save 1/2 cup of cooking water. Mix dressing ingredients together and stuff into body cavities, skewer cavities shut and place breast side down on baking rack in large roasting pan. Rub turkey with 1/4 cup of softened butter. Roast turkey uncovered, at 325 for 1 1/2 hours basting every 20 minutes with butter and drippings. Turn turkey so breast side is up and continue basting and baking until leg joint moves easily (30 minutes per pound).

*Many recipes for domestic turkey will adapt well to wild turkey meat. Keep in mind that wild turkey has less fat and will dry out quicker. Baste often. Draping bacon strips over the bird also helps.*

# TURKEY

## WILD RICE SOUP

leftover turkey carcass and meat

9 cups water

4 cups cooked wild rice

pinch of parsley

1/2 tsp. thyme

1/4 onion chopped

2 small carrots, chopped

1 bay leaf

salt and pepper to taste

Break apart carcass. Place in pot with water and bring to boil. Add remaining ingredients except for wild rice. Simmer for approximately two hours.

Remove carcass, stripping off any remaining meat to put back into soup. Skim off any excessive fat. Add wild rice.

Simmer for an additional 20 minutes. Any leftover soup may be frozen.

## WOODLANDS WILD TURKEY

1 turkey dressed

juice of one lemon

1/3 cup margarine, butter

3 tablespoons flour

3 apples, sliced

1/2 cup chopped celery

1/2 cup cooking oil

salt and pepper to taste

Prepare bird by thoroughly cleaning inside and out with cold water. Lightly rub salt and pepper on inside of turkey.

Mix margarine, flour and pepper and additional seasonings (optional) into paste and spread all over outside of turkey. Stuff turkey with apples and celery pieces mixed together. Tie turkey up.

Baste turkey with oil and lemon mixture. Roast approximately two hours for birds under 10 pounds, 2 1/2 hours for larger birds. Baste often with oil and lemon mixture and pan juices.

# STUFFED
# GAMEHEN

| | |
|---|---|
| 6 game hens | 6 tbsp. butter |
| 1 cup wild rice | 2 1/2 cup water |
| 1 tsp. salt | 4 strips bacon |
| 5 scallions, sliced | 1/2 lb. mushrooms |
| 1 tbsp. butter | 1 cup hazelnuts, chopped |

Season hens with salt and pepper. Wash wild rice, add water and salt and bring to a boil, reduce heat, simmer until water is absorbed. Brown bacon in skillet, saute scallions, and coarsely chopped mushrooms, combine with wild rice and remaining ingredients.

Rub hens with butter, stuff with stuffing. Roast at 350 F. for 2 to 2 1/2 hours, basting frequently with butter and drippings.

# PARTRIDGE

The partridge are land birds with small heads and bills, and long legs. They are brown in color and have a ruff around the neck and fan-shaped tail. These birds are chicken-like and nest on the ground.

They are non-migratory, although they tend to wander irregularly in winter. They are found throughout the northern hemisphere and can survive the winter months because of their ability to feed in trees. This family of birds are superb dinner fare.

Typically, these birds weigh around one pound, dressed weight.

# BAKED PARTRIDGE

4 partridge, dressed
1 small clove of garlic, chopped
1 small onion, halved
1 tbsp. celery, chopped

1/4 tsp. pepper
1 tsp. salt
1/3 cup butter
1/2 cup water

Cut up partridge using the breasts and thighs. Brown lightly in butter with onion and garlic. Place in small roasting pan and add water and chopped celery. Bake, covered, at 350 F for 1 1/2 hours. Baste frequently to prevent dryness.

# PARTRIDGE
# WITH GRAPE JUICE

*4 partridges, dressed*  
*1/2 cup bacon fat*  
*1 pint grape juice*  
*1 whole clove*

*1 bay leaf*  
*cornstarch*  
*water*

Heat bacon fat in skillet and lightly brown the partridge. Add grape juice, clove and bay leaf. Cover and simmer for 50 minutes. Remove meat to a hot platter. Discard bay leaf and clove and thicken liquid with cornstarch and water. Pour sauce over partridge and serve.

# LEMON FLAVORED
# PARTRIDGE

*4 partridge, cut into pieces*  
*salt and pepper to taste*  
*1/4 cup lemon juice*  
*1/3 cup oil*

*1 clove garlic, minced*  
*1 tsp. parsley flakes*  
*2 tsp. oregano*

Salt and pepper partridge pieces. In a bowl, mix lemon juice, oil, garlic, parsley and oregano. Dip each piece of meat in mixture and place on a broiler pan. Broil 15 to 20 minutes on each side. Baste occasionally with lemon oil mixture.

## PARTRIDGE CASSEROLE

*2 partridge cut into*
*serving pieces*
*1/4 cup flour*
*1 tsp. salt*

*1 onion, sliced*
*5 tbsp. butter or margarine*
*1 cup canned mushroom soup*
*1 1/2 cups boiling water*

Mix flour, salt, and pepper. Dredge partridge in flour until well coated. Melt butter in heavy frying pan and brown partridge on all sides. When browned remove from pan and put pieces into well buttered casserole dish. Pour over mushroom soup that has been mixed with boiling water. Add onions and seasonings. Simmer for 1 1/2 hours.

# PARTRIDGE
# AND WILD RICE DRESSING

| | |
|---|---|
| *2 partridges* | *1 large onion, diced* |
| *3/4 lb. sweet sausage* | *1 clove garlic, minced* |
| *1/2 cup uncooked wild rice* | *1/2 cup water* |
| *2 slices white bread* | *2 eggs, beaten* |
| *1/2 cup milk* | *3 thin slices salt pork* |
| *1/4 cup olive oil* | *1/4 tsp. salt* |
| *7 tbsp. butter* | *1/4 tsp. pepper* |
| *1 oz. salt pork, diced* | *1/4 cup chicken stock (or boiled giblets)* |

Remove casing from sausage and cut into small pieces. Soak rice in warm water for 15 minutes and then drain. Cook in salted water for 20 minutes and drain again. Soak bread in milk; drain, squeeze and shred. In a skillet, heat 3 tablespoons oil, 4 tablespoons butter and add salt pork and onions. Cook until golden brown. Add sausage and cook 20 minutes. Add water to skillet, cover and cook for 3 minutes. Remove from heat and let cool.

Then add to skillet shredded bread, beaten eggs, rice and garlic. Mix well. Stuff birds. Oil roasting pan and place birds breast down. Roast at 450 F for 10 minutes and turn down to 300 F and roast for 1 hour.

## PARTRIDGE STEW

| | |
|---|---|
| *2 partridges, cut into serving pieces* | *1 tsp. poultry seasoning* |
| *4 tbsp. butter* | *1 can chicken and rice soup* |
| *1 onion, finely chopped* | *1/4 cup water* |
| *1 carrot, thinly sliced* | *salt and pepper to taste* |
| *1 tsp. parsley, chopped* | *3 tbsp. flour* |

Brown partridge pieces in butter. In a large saucepan, add onion, carrot, parsley and poultry seasoning. Cook slowly. Stir in flour, gradually adding soup, water and mushrooms. Season with salt and pepper. Simmer, covered until tender.

## PARTRIDGE
## WITH BREAD SAUCE

*4 partridge breasts*
*4 strips bacon*
*1/2 cup water*

Wrap each breast in a piece of bacon and place in a small roasting pan. Add 1/2 cup water, cover and roast for 30 minutes at 350 F.

## BREAD SAUCE:

2 cups milk
1 small onion, diced
dash of nutmeg

1 tbsp. butter
1/2 tsp. salt
1 cup light bread crumbs

Pour milk in a saucepan. Add onions and bring to a boil. Add bread crumbs, salt, nutmeg and butter; reduce heat, stir and simmer for 15 minutes. Pour over partridge and serve.

## PARTRIDGE PIE

1 cup cooked partridge, cubed
3/4 cup peas
1 cup well seasoned gravy
1/2 cup carrots, cooked
biscuit dough

Combine partridge, vegetables and gravy into casserole dish. Top with biscuit dough. Bake at 450 F for 15 to 20 minutes.

# PHEASANT AND QUAIL

These birds are chicken - like and they take their food from the ground. They suffer in winter because of their inability to feed above the snow cover. All these birds are noted for their beautiful appearance.

Members of this family include the Bobwhite, California, Mountain and Gambel's Quail. Ring-Necked Pheasants are very tasty if you are be fortunate enough to bag one. Ring-necks typically dress out at 1 1/2 to 2 1/2 pounds; quail at five to seven ounces.

✳

# CREAM-ROASTED
# PHEASANT

*pheasant, dressed*          *pepper*
*flour*                      *butter*
*salt*                       *cream*

Cut pheasant into serving pieces. Wash and pat dry. Dredge with flour, salt and pepper. Fry in butter until light to brown on both sides. Place in a roasting pan and add enough cream to cover the pieces. Bake at 350 F until tender about 20 minutes per pound.

✳

# 123.
## ROAST WILD PHEASANT

1/2 cup grape jelly

1/2 cup water

1 pheasant, dressed

1 cup celery, chopped

1 cup onion, chopped

salt and pepper to taste

1 cup margarine

lemon juice

Wash and pat dry meat. Wipe cavity well with lemon juice. Combine celery and onion mixture. Stuff pheasant with this but do not close cavity. Fold wings over the back, tuck in the neck skin and hold with a skewer; tie legs together. Place breast side up on a rack in a roasting pan. Add 1/2 cup water, cover with foil and roast at 350 F until tender. Allow 15 to 20 minutes per pound. When meat is cooked, remove foil and add 1/2 cup grape jelly to drippings. Cook uncovered for 15 minutes, basting frequently.

## QUAIL AND PEPPERS

1/2 cup oil

1/2 cup onion, chopped

4 quail, quartered

1/2 tsp. salt

1/8 tsp. cayenne

1 cup tomatoes

2 sweet red peppers, sliced thin

2 green peppers, sliced thin

Heat oil in large dutch oven. Saute onion until brown. Add quail and cook on both sides until brown. Sprinkle salt and cayenne over quail pieces. Add tomatoes and cook covered for 30 minutes on low heat. Add peppers. Cook for an additional 20 minutes or until peppers are tender.

# PHEASANT
# WITH WILD RICE STUFFING

| | |
|---|---|
| 1 pheasant, dressed | 1/2 cup onion, chopped |
| lemon juice | 1/4 cup celery, chopped |
| 1 1/2 cups wild rice | 1/4 cup margarine |
| 3 cups boiling water | 1 tbsp. poultry seasoning |
| 2 cups mushrooms, stems | 1/2 cup stewed tomatoes |
| and pieces | 1 tbsp. bacon fat |

1 tsp. salt

Wash and pat dry the meat. Rub cavity well with lemon juice. Wash rice in cold water, drain, then place rice in a sauce pan. Cover with boiling water; add salt and simmer for 55 to 60 minutes. Add more water when necessary. When rice is tender, drain.

In a skillet over low heat, melt margarine and bacon fat. Saute mushrooms, onions and celery until tender. In a mixing bowl, pour in tomatoes and seasonings. Mix rice and mushroom mixture into this. Stuff bird, then place on a rack in a roasting pan. Pour over 2 cups of water. Cover bird loosely with tin foil and bake at 350 F until tender.

✳

# BRAISED QUAIL

**4 quail**                                    **1/4 cup cider**

**6 tbsp. butter**

Place 1 tablespoon of butter in the cavity of each quail and close opening with skewer. Melt remaining 2 tablespoons of butter in heavy skillet and brown the birds over low heat. Place in casserole dish. Add cider and cover and bake for 20 minutes or until the birds are tender.

# PIGEONS AND DOVES

This family of birds is noted for their small heads, small bills and short legs. They are extremely fast flying birds, with pointed wings. They feed on the ground on weed seeds and waste grain. Pigeons and doves are prolific. Found in almost all areas of North America and Mexico. They are prized table meat- average dressed weight per bird is four to six ounces.

## DOVE CASSEROLE

*4 to 5 doves, dressed*       *1 can cream of chicken soup*
*1 carrot, grated*       *1 cup peas*
*1 celery stalk, chopped*       *1/2 cup condensed milk*
*1/4 tsp. rosemary*       *salt and pepper to taste*
*2 tbsp. fat, melted*

Place doves in a casserole dish. Sprinkle grated carrots and celery over doves. Mix together, remaining ingredients and pour over doves. Cover and bake at 375 F for about 2 hours.

# DOVES WITH MUSHROOM SAUCE

8 to 10 doves, dressed
1/4 cup butter
1 can mushroom gravy
1 (10 oz.) can whole mushrooms
1/2 tsp. sage
1 onion, sliced
1/4 cup dry red wine (optional)
flour
salt and pepper to taste

Dredge the doves in flour.  Melt butter in a heavy skillet and sear the doves.   Add onions and saute until soft.   Combine remaining ingredients; mix thoroughly.  Pour over doves and add enough water to cover doves completely.   Cover skillet and cook over low heat for  1  to  1 1/2 hours.

# PIGEON PIE

Pastry for double
   pie crust
5 pigeons, cleaned and washed
2 tsp. salt
1/2 onion, minced
1 stalk celery, chopped
3 whole cloves
1/2 lb. salt pork, diced
cornstarch
potato, thinly sliced

Cut pigeons in half and place in a large cooking pot along with the salt pork.  Cover with water and bring to a boil.  Skim surface.  Add salt, onion, celery, cloves and simmer for 20 minutes. Take out the meat and thicken the liquid with cornstarch.

Remove bones from the pigeon and cut larger pieces of meat into small chunks. Line baking dish with pastry and cover bottom with thinly sliced raw potatoes. Add the meat pieces and cover with another layer of thinly sliced potatoes. Pour in liquid and then cover with pastry. Make two slits in center of pie to allow steam to escape. Bake for 30 minutes at 350 F.

# PIGEONS WITH
# SAUSAGE STUFFING

6 pigeons

salt

1 lb. sausage meat

2 onions, chopped

1 cup, potatoes, mashed

salt and pepper

6 tbsp. butter, melted

6 slices bacon

1 1/2 cups chicken stock

1/2 cup white wine

1/2 tsp. sage

Rub pigeons with salt inside and out. In a skillet, brown the sausage meat over low heat. Pour off fat and add onions, and saute until soft. Stir in mashed potatoes and season with sage, salt and pepper. Stuff mixture into bird's cavity and truss. Place birds breast side up, on rack in a roasting pan and brush with melted butter. Cut each bacon slice in half and attach to breasts by securing with tooth picks. Roast 20 minutes, basting and turning birds twice. Remove the bacon and roast 20 minutes longer until breasts are brown and the birds are tender. Place birds on a hot platter and keep warm. Pour the fat from the roasting pan and add the stock and wine and bring to a boil. Simmer until volume is reduced to half. Serve sauce in gravy boat.

# CHAPTER FOUR
## · FISH AND SEAFOOD ·

Catching fish with a hook and line, as in modern sport-fishing was not the preferred method of most tribes due to its relative inefficiency.

Fish were harvested in a number of different ways, most of which are considered unsportsmanlike or even illegal now. Elaborate weirs, traps built of saplings and interwoven with twigs, were built at strategic places in the mouths of rivers and low tide areas. Other tribes netted fish with nets made of handworked natural fibers. Bowhunting and spearing of fish was common among almost all tribes. Certain tribes developed herbal based poisons which, when introduced into a lake or small stream, stunned fish and caused them to float helplessly to the surface where they could be gathered easily. Nightfishing, using fish oil lanterns for illumination, was also practiced by native people.

Fish should be cleaned (see Cleaning and Dressing Chapter) immediately after catching and stored in a cold place until ready to use or frozen if they are not going to be eaten the same day.

In order to tell if the fish has cooked sufficiently, the meat should flake at the touch of a fork, usually in about 10 minutes.

## TROUT WITH ALMONDS

*1 fresh trout, per person*  
*salt and pepper*  
*juice of 2 lemons*  

*4 tbsp. butter*  
*1/2 cup blanched sliced almonds*  
*parsley*

Rub trout with butter and season with salt and pepper. Pour lemon juice over fish. Place in a greased baking dish and bake at 350 F for 10 minutes per pound. Meanwhile melt butter in a saucepan. Add almonds and cook until brown. Pour butter and browned almonds over trout and garnish with parsley. Serve.

## CORN BREAD
## STUFFED TROUT

1 (3 lb) trout, cleaned

1 cup crumbled corn bread

1 cup soft bread crumbs

1/2 cup celery, chopped

1/4 cup onion, finely chopped

1/2 tsp. salt

1/4 tsp. sage

pepper

1/4 cup water

3 tbsp. melted butter

2 tbsp. green pepper, chopped

Season fish generously with salt. Place into a well greased shallow baking pan. Mix crumbled corn bread, soft bread crumbs, celery, onion, green pepper, 1/2 tsp. salt, sage and pepper. Gradually add water to bread mixture tossing to coat. Stuff fish loosely with mixture. Brush fish generously with melted butter and cover with foil. Bake at 350 F for 45 - 60 minutes.

## TOASTED CHEESE
## FILLETS

8 trout fillets

salt and pepper

1 cup corn meal

8 slices bread

8 slices cheese

salad dressing

1 cup cooking oil

# 131.

## PICKEREL

It has a perch-like structure with 2 dorsal fins, a longish pike-like head and, many sharp canine teeth. The scales are small and rough. Colour varies but is usually a motted dark olive and brassy. The belly is yellowish or white. Medium size fish reach lengths under 3 ft. and weighs less than 20 lbs. They are also found in the Great Lakes region.

## PIKE

Similiar in features to the muskellunge, the size is usually under 4 ft. and under 40 lbs. It has a long pointed head, forminable teeth and fine scales. The dorsal and anal fins are located near the tail, opposite one another. They are usually dark gray on the back, grayish-silver with roundish or squarish spots on the sides and white on the belly. They are found in northern North America.

## SALMON

They vary in size from 15-100 lbs. They are found in the Atlantic and Pacific Oceans, rivers that flow into them, and The Great Lakes and their tributaries. They are delicious to eat.

## SMELT

Smelt are small slender fish. They have a translucent greenish back with silvery sides. They rarely exceed 10 inches in length. They are found from Virginia northward to the Gulf of the St. Lawrence.

## LARGE LAKE TROUT

A large lake trout has very dark to pale gray back and sometimes has greenish sides. It is profusely spotted. They can grow to a very large size weighing up to 80 lbs. It is found in deep water lakes from The Great Lakes north to Labrador, Hudson Bay and Alaska.

Salt and pepper fillets then coat with corn meal.  Heat cooking oil until a droplet of water bounces off of it.  Drop in fillets.  At the same time, toast bread.  When fillets are golden brown and crisp on bottom, turn over and lay a slice of cheese on the browned side.  Continue frying until cheese begins to melt.  Drain on a paper towel.  Place each fillet on a slice of hot buttered toast and top with salad dressing.

⁕

# BARBECUED
# STUFFED TROUT

*8 - 10 lbs. trout, cleaned*          *salad oil*
*salt and pepper*                     *1/2 cup butter, melted*
*\*Garden Vegetable Stuffing*          *1/4 cup lemon juice*

Wash fish in cold water and pat dry.  Rub cavity with salt and pepper.  Stuff with "Garden Vegetable Stuffing".  Close opening with skewers. Brush fish with salad oil. Place fish into a wire basket 4 - 6 inches from coals.  Cook for 45 minutes, turning 3 times and basting with the 1/2 cup butter and 1/4 cup lemon juice mixture.

⁕

## 133. BASS

The bass is an abundant fish. They can be found in sluggish or clear water depending on the variety. The colour is dark green on the back, dull greenish-silver on the sides and pale below. Weight of fish is about 2-3 lbs. It is found in the Great Lake region.

## CARP

Carp is a large coarse fish with a saw edged spine on the dorsal and anal fin. It has 2 pairs of barbels at the mouth. It is a dusky greenish or brownish on the back and sides; yellowish on the lower sides and belly and reddish on the fins. It reaches a length of 2 ft. or more and weights of more than 7 lbs.

## CATFISH

The catfish has a boney ridge from head to dorsal fin. It has 4 barbels around its mouth. It's colour varies from dark yellowish brown to black. It reaches a length of 12 - 18 inches and seldom weighs more than 1 or 2 pounds. It is found in the Great Lakes region, and is very good to eat.

## EEL

It has a long snake-like form with a large mouth, projecting lower jaw, and will develop pectaral fins. The scales are small and imbedded. It is variable in colour; running from brown to yellowish-olive with a paler underside. It may reach lengths of 4 - 5 ft. and weigh only 7 lbs.

## MUSKIE (Muskellunge)

Muskie has a long pointed head, formidable teeth and fine scales. The dorsel and anal fins are located opposite one another, near the tail. They are usually dark gray on the back; grayish-silver with round or squarish blackish spots on their sides and a white belly. The length is 4 ft. and weighs 50 lbs. They are found in the Great Lake region.

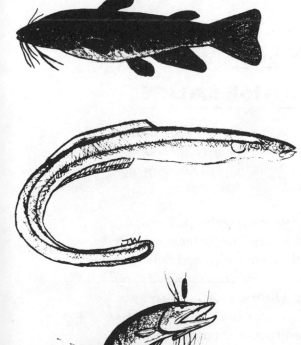

# ***GARDEN VEGETABLE
# STUFFING

| | |
|---|---|
| 1/4 cup butter | 1 1/2 tbsp. lemon juice |
| 1 cup onion, chopped fine | 1 egg |
| 2 cups dry bread cubes | 1 clove garlic, minced |
| 1 cup coarsely shredded carrots | 2 tbsp. salt |
| 1 cup chopped mushrooms | 1/4 tsp. marjoram |
| 1/2 cup parsley flakes | 1/4 tsp. pepper |

Saute onion in butter until tender. Remove from heat and mix in remaining ingredients.

✳

# FRIED SMELTS
# WITH HOLLANDAISE SAUCE

| | |
|---|---|
| smelts | 2 eggs, beaten |
| salt | 1 cup bread crumbs |
| 1 cup flour | fat for frying |

To clean smelt, make a cut up the stomach with a pair of sharp scissors. Remove the intestines. Wash and pat dry. Dredge the smelt with salt and flour mixture. Dip the smelt in the beaten eggs and roll in the bread crumbs. Fry in hot fat, hot enough to brown a cube of bread in 60 seconds. After putting in the fish, reduce the heat so that the fish may be sufficiently cooked without becoming too brown. Cook for 3 or 4 minutes or until nicely browned. Drain. Garnish with lemon or parsley and serve with hollandaise sauce.

## HOLLANDAISE SAUCE

3 tbsp. butter
dash of cayenne
2 egg yolks, beaten

3 cups boiling water
1/4 tsp. salt
1 tbsp. lemon juice

In a saucepan, cream the butter and egg yolks. Add seasonings and mix in the water. Simmer until thick; stirring constantly. Remove from heat and mix in the lemon juice.

## POACHED LAKE TROUT

3 to 4 lbs. lake trout, fillets
1/2 cup milk
1/2 cup water
4 slices lemon
1/2 tsp. allspice

1/2 tsp. salt
1 sprig parsley
*2 cups white sauce
2 hard boiled eggs, chopped

In a frying pan combine fish, milk, water, lemon slices, allspice, salt and parsley. Cover and cook over low heat until tender. Place on platter.

Combine hot white sauce, lemon juice and chopped hard boiled eggs. Pour over fish and serve.

## *WHITE SAUCE

*4 tbsp. butter*
*4 tbsp. flour*
*2 cups milk*

In a saucepan melt butter.  Stir in flour until it is all absorbed. Slowly stir in the milk.  Cook, stirring constantly until thickened.

❋

## FISH CAKES

*These are nothing like the kind bought in stores.*
*The difference in taste is like night and day.*

*2 cups cooked trout*
*3 cups mashed potatoes*
*4 tbsp. butter*

*1 egg, well beaten*
*1 onion, chopped fine*
*salt and pepper to taste*

Combine all ingredients together and shape into balls.  Dip balls into the beaten egg, and roll in bread crumbs.  Fry in a hot skillet using just enough fat to keep them from burning.  Turn often so they will cook evenly.  Serve hot.

❋

## TROUT SCALLOPS

| | |
|---|---|
| 1 lb. cooked trout | 1 tsp. chives |
| 1 tbsp. butter | 1 tsp. parsley |
| 2 tbsp. water | 1/2 cup bread crumbs |
| 1/2 cup milk | salt and pepper to taste |

2 eggs

Melt butter and add the cooked trout. Season with salt and pepper. Pour water over fish and simmer in saucepan with lid on for 10 minutes. Beat eggs and add milk. Stir into fish adding chopped chives and chopped parsley. Pour into oven dish. Top with bread crumbs. Bake at 350 F for 15 minutes.

＊

## FISH CHEEKS

fish cheeks from pickerel or lake trout
1 egg, beaten
salt and pepper to taste
6 - 8 crackers, crumbled

The cheeks of pickerel and lake trout are large enough to use. They are boneless, skinless and considered a delicacy. Wash well. Add salt and pepper to egg. Dip cheek into the egg and then roll in the crumbs. Fry over medium heat in bacon fat or oil.

# GREAT LAKES
# FRIED WHITEFISH

3 lbs. whitefish                          1 tsp. salt
1 cup cornmeal                        1/2 tsp. lemon juice
4 tbsp. bacon fat                      1 1/2 tsp. worcestershire sauce

Mix cornmeal thoroughly with salt and pepper. Roll fish in the cornmeal mixture. Heat bacon fat in a heavy skillet. Brown fish 6 to 8 minutes on each side or until fish flakes easily with a fork. Mix lemon juice with worcestershire sauce and pour over fish when serving.

✳

# WHITEFISH AND
# NOODLE CASSEROLE

2 lbs. whitefish fillets                    1/4 tsp. pepper
8 ounces noodles, cooked             1/4 tsp. basil
1 medium onion, sliced                2 1/2 cups tomato sauce
                    1/4 tsp. salt

Grease casserole dish and add cooked noodles and tomato sauce. Put in sliced onions and then fish fillets. Sprinkle with salt, pepper and sweet basil. Bake at 300 F for 30 minutes or until done to taste.

✳

## JELLIED BAKED
## WHITE FISH

*1 cup flaked white fish (baked)*
*1 1/2 cups chopped vegetables (cooked)*
*1/4 cup mild vinegar*     *1 pkg. lemon jelly powder*
*1 3/4 cups hot tomato juice*     *1/4 tsp. tabasco sauce*

Dissolve jelly powder in hot tomato juice and tabasco sauce. Add vinegar. Chill. When slightly thickened, mix in flaked white fish and vegetables. Garnish with deviled eggs, cheese balls, pickles or olives.

## QUICK
## BASS FRY

*2 lbs. bass fillets*     *1 cup pancake mix*
*1 cup milk*     *clear fat for frying*

Dip fillets into milk then dredge with pancake mix. Fry in hot fat. Drain cooked pieces on paper towels.

# BASS
# WITH HERBS

1 bass, cleaned

4 tbsp. butter

1 small clove garlic, chopped

2 onion slices, minced

1/2 tsp. parsley

1 tsp. tarragon leaves, chopped

salt and pepper to taste

2 tbsp. lemon juice

Prepare bass for pan frying. Melt butter in a skillet. Add garlic, onion, parsley and tarragon. Simmer 2 minutes. Season fish with salt and pepper then cook gently in the herb-butter mixture until tender. Remove bass and place on a hot serving dish. Add lemon juice to sauce in skillet, reheat and pour over fish.

＊

# DANDY PERCH

10 -12 small perch, cleaned

butter and vegetable oil

1 garlic clove, chopped fine

white wine vinegar

1 bunch dandelion shoots

Using equals amounts of butter and oil, saute young dandelion shoots with garlic. Remove and set aside in a warm oven. Use the same oil to fry fish quickly, a few minutes on each side. Sprinkle wine vinegar sparingly over fish. Serve covered with dandelion shoots.

＊

# FISH CHOWDER

1 lb. pickerel fillets    1 cup boiling water
1/4 lb. bacon       3 cups milk
3 onions, sliced     1 tbsp. butter
4 small potatoes, pared, cubed  2 tbsp. chopped parsley
1 tsp. salt

Chop bacon. Fry bacon slowly in a heavy fry pan or saucepan until crisp and golden brown. Lift out bacon bits and set aside. Add onions to fat and cook until transparent. Add potatoes, salt and water. Cut fish into 2 inch squares. Drop over potatoes, cover and simmer until potatoes are tender and fish flakes, approximately 20 minutes. Add milk and heat. More salt may be aded if necessary. Just before serving, drop butter, bacon and parsley into chowder; do not stir.

✹

# FISH A LA CREME

4 lbs. pickerel        2 tbsp. salt
water

Place fish into a large saucepan; cover with salted water and bring to a boil. Reduce heat; cover and simmer for approximately 1 hour. Drain and place on a platter.

---

## SAUCE:

3 cups milk
2 tbsp. flour
2 tbsp. lemon juice
1 small onion, chopped

1 tbsp. parsley
dash of nutmeg
salt and pepper
1 tbsp. butter

Blend milk and flour in a saucepan thoroughly. Stir in lemon juice, onion, parsley, nutmeg, salt and pepper. Place saucepan over medium heat and stir until thickened. Mix in butter. Pour over fish and serve.

# MACARONI FISH PIE

1 lb. pickerel
3/4 cup macaroni

water
1 tsp. salt

### CHEESE SAUCE:

2 tbsp. butter
1/4 cu all-purpose flour
1 1/4 cups milk

dash of dry mustard
salt, pepper, garlic
3/4 cup grated cheddar cheese

Cook macaroni according to package directions. Meanwhile simmer fish in a little salted water until tender. Remove fish and break into large flakes. Heat butter in a pan then stir in flour and cook 2 - 3 minutes over low heat. Gradually add milk and seasonings. Bring to a boil and cook until thickened. Add grated cheese, but do not reboil. Place drained macaroni and fish into a hot dish and top with cheese sauce. Place under broiler for 2 - 3 minutes or until top is bubbly.

# BAKED STUFFED

# PICKEREL

| | |
|---|---|
| *1 - 4 lbs. pickerel* | *1 cup brown rice, cooked* |
| *salt and pepper* | *1 tbsp. worcestershire sauce* |
| *2 cups spinach, chopped* | *melted butter* |
| *1/2 cup onion, chopped* | *paprika if desired* |
| | *1/2 cup cheese, grated* |

Clean and scale pickerel leaving head and tail intact. Sprinkle inside of fish with salt and pepper.

## Stuffing:

Mix together spinach, onion, cheese, rice and worcestershire sauce. Stuff fish and skewer the opening closed. Brush all sides of fish with melted butter. Season with salt and pepper. Sprinkle with paprika, if desired, place into a baking dish and cover with foil. Bake at 350 F for 30 -35 minutes.

NOTE:

Any extra stuffing can be cooked around the fish.

# OVEN COOKED
# WHITEFISH

4 whitefish fillets
1/2 cup milk
1 1/2 tsp. salt

1/2 tsp. pepper
1/2 cup cornmeal
1/3 cup cooking oil

Dip fillets in their milk mixed with salt and pepper, then coat with cornmeal. Heat 1/2 of the oil in a baking pan. Arrange fillets and sprinkle with remaining oil. Bake at 475 F for 20 minutes, or until fish has browned and flakes easily. Serve with your favorite sauce.

✳

# WHITEFISH
# WITH EGG SAUCE

3 lbs. whitefish, cleaned
water

2 tbsp. salt
1 tbsp. pepper

Lay fish split side down in a large skillet that has a tight fitting lid. Add enough water to cover fish then add salt and butter. Cover and simmer 45 minutes. Do not boil. Drain.

## SAUCE:

2 tbsp. butter
1 tbsp. flour

1 cup milk
3 hard boiled eggs, sliced thin

Melt butter in a saucepan and stir in flour until well blended. Slowly mix in milk and bring to a boil. Stir in eggs. Remove from heat. Pour sauce over fish and serve.

## BAKED FISH

| | |
|---|---|
| 2 lbs. fresh fillets | 1 small tomato, chopped |
| 2 tbsp. oil | 1/2 cup water |
| 1/2 cup onion, chopped | 1 tsp. dill seed |
| 1/4 cup celery, chopped | 1/2 tsp. salt |
| 1/4 cup green pepper, chopped | 1 tbsp. lemon juice |

In a skillet, add oil, onion, celery, green pepper and carrots. Cook until tender. Stir in tomato, water, dill and bring to a boil. Then simmer for 10 minutes. Scatter 1/2 of this mixture in a baking dish, place fish on top and add remaining mixture. Sprinkle with salt, pepper and lemon juice. Bake at 400 F for 20 minutes.

## BAKED FISH
## WITH CHILI SAUCE

*Fish, whole or filleted*
*2 tbsp. chili sauce*
*1 tbsp. tomato sauce*
*1/2 cup sour cream*
*1 tbsp. chopped parsley*

Place cleaned fish (skin removed) in a greased casserole dish. Mix chili, tomato sauce and cream together and pour over fish. Sprinkle with parsley. Bake covered at 350 F for 25 minutes.

# WONDERFUL

# FISH FILLETS

2 1/2 lb. fresh fish  
1/2 tbsp. pepper  
2 eggs, beaten

1 tsp. salt  
2 tbsp. rice  
1 cup evaporated milk, chilled

3 tbsp. fat, melted

Chop fillets and add melted fat, eggs, rice, salt and pepper. Whip the chilled milk stiffly and fold in. Bake at 325 F for 45 minutes in a greased 1 1/2 quart casserole dish.

# SIMPLY

# TRADITIONAL FISH

4 portions or a whole fish  
3 small onions, sliced  
2 apples, chopped  
1 1/4 cups cider  
2 bay leaves  
lemon

Season fish with salt and pepper. Place in a greased casserole dish. Add onions and the apples. Then pour cider and bay leaves over dish.

# MARINADED
# WHOLE FISH
# IN FOIL

*4 -5 lbs. whole fish dressed and head removed.*

## *MARINADE:*

| | |
|---|---|
| *1 clove garlic, minced* | *1/4 cup chopped onion* |
| *1 tsp. oregano* | *dash freshly ground pepper* |
| *1 tsp. salt* | *1/2 cup corn oil* |
| *1/2 tsp. basil* | *1/4 cup lemon juice* |
| *1/2 tsp. thyme* | |

   Mix garlic, oregano, salt, basil, thyme and pepper.  Stir in corn oil, lemon juice and onions.  Set aside.

   Tear off a sheet of extra heavy foil wrap twice the length of the fish, plus 3 inches.  Place fish in foil.  Pour marinade over fish.  Bring extending half of foil over fish and seal the 3 sides with double folds.  Refrigerate for 1 hour.

   Place on grill approximately 5 inches from heat, turn once or twice until fish flakes easy with fork.  Cook for 45 to 60 minutes.

# SPECIAL

# FISH CHOWDER

| | |
|---|---|
| 1/2 lb. fish, fresh or frozen | 1 tsp. salt |
| 1 tbsp. margarine | 1/2 tsp. pepper |
| 1 small onion, chopped | 3/4 cup elbow macaroni |
| 1 stalk celery, chopped | 1 1/2 cups milk |
| 1 medium carrot, thinly sliced | 1 tbsp. parsley |

Cut fish into bite-sized pieces and set aside. Saute celery, onions and carrots in margarine for 5 minutes. Add boiling water, salt and pepper. Cover and simmer for 10 minutes.

Add macaroni and simmer for 5 minutes. Add fish and simmer covered for 10 minutes longer. Stir occasionally. Add milk and heat without boiling.

Garnish with parsley leaves and serve.

*Thaw fish in milk.*
*The milk draws out the frozen taste and provides a fresh caught taste.*

# SALMON WITH
# AVOCADO SAUCE

4 salmon steaks                          3 tbsp. butter
1-2 cup chicken broth                    1/2 cup
                    chopped onion

Melt butter, sautee onions until translucent.  Add salmon and saute one minute on each side.  Cover with broth , bring to a gentle boil, turn heat down to low and poach 7 minutes more. Remove salmon to seving platter and keep warm.  Reduce liquid to 1/2 cup and set aside for avocado sauce.

# AVOCADO SAUCE

2 tbsp. butter                          1 1/2 tbsp. flour
1/2 cup hot milk                        1/2 cup salmon broth
3 tbsp. lemon juice                     dash tabasco sauce
1 ripe avocado, chopped                 salt and pepper to taste

Melt butter in saucepan, stir in flour, cooking 2 minutes.  Add milk and broth, simmer 5 minutes, stirring constantly until thickened. Pour into blender, add remaining ingredients and puree.  Serve over steaks.

## DILLY FRIED SALMON

6 Salmon
1 1/2 tsp. salt
1/4 tsp. pepper

1/2 cup butter
2 teaspoon dill
3 tsp. lemon juice

Cut fish almost through lengthwise and spread open. Sprinkle with salt and pepper. Melt butter in 10" skillet, add dill. Place two fish flesh-side sown into hot dill butter, fry 2 to 3 minutes over moderate heat. Remove fish to a warm plate and repeat with remaining fish. When last fish is cooked, lower heat to simmer and stir in lemon juice. Pour sauce over fish.

## SALMON BAKED IN KELP

3 fresh kelp fronds
2 cup kelp stems
3 medium onions, chopped
2 eggs, beaten

1 large salmon
10 cups bread crumbs
1/2 cup butter
salt, pepper, garlic to taste

Wash kelp in fresh salt water. Cut off the stems and chop them. Saute onions and kelp in butter until onion is translucent. Add crumbs, eggs and seasoning to make stuffing. Clean fish, pack stuffing inside it, wrap in a layer of kelp, then foil. Bury fish in hot coals and bake approximately 3 hours.

# GRILLED
# SALMON STEAKS

6 salmon steaks
salt and pepper to taste

30 juniper berries
lemon wedges

Crush berries slightly, press halfway down in steaks. Grill over coals for 3 minutes on each side. Season with salt and pepper. Serve with lemon wedges.

# SALMON WITH
# SKUNK CABBAGE

1 medium salmon
2 tbsp. butter
salt and pepper

4 skunk cabbage leaves
1 small onion, minced
1 lemon

Saute onion in butter until translucent, add salt and pepper. Rub salmon with cut lemon and baste inside and out with butter mixture. Wrap in skunk cabbage leaves and bake over charcoal for 2 hours.

# SALMON WITH WATERCRESS

4 salmon fillets                    4 tbsp. butter

2 cup mushrooms                 4 scallions, sliced thinly

1/2 tsp. salt                         1/4 tsp. pepper

1 1/2 tsp. garlic, minced        1 cup cream

1 bunch watercress

Melt butter in saucepan, brush melted butter on fillets and set aside. Saute mushrooms, scallions and garlic until scallions are translucent; add cream and seasonings and reduce until sauce coats a spoon. Mince watercress and add to sauce. Grill fillets five minutes per side. Spoon sauce over salmon and serve.

# POACHED SALMON
# WITH MUSHROOMS

6 (1") salmon steaks             6 medium mushrooms, sliced

2 tsp. minced parsley            2 scallions, sliced

1 sweet red pepper               2 cup chicken broth

1 tsp. salt                            1/4 tsp. pepper

Simmer all ingredients except salmon in chicken broth for 10 minutes. Cool to room temperature. Place salmon steaks in a large skillet, cover with broth and simmer for 15 to 20 minutes. Remove to warm plate. Boil broth down to one cup. Serve each steak topped with broth mixture. Salmon may be served hot or cold.

## SALMON CAKES

1 lbs. flaked salmon   10 juniper berries, crushed
1/3 cup corn meal     2 eggs, lightly beaten
2/3 cup milk       salt and pepper to taste

  Mix all ingredients together, form into thin patties and fry until browned on both sides.

## SMOKED SALMON WITH EGGS

6 eggs         1/8 tsp. pepper
1 tbsp. minced chives     2 tbsp. butter
1/2 lb. smoked salmon in julienne strips

  Beat the eggs with the pepper until frothy.  Stir in the minced chives.  Melt butter in a large skillet, pour in the egg mixture, add the smoked salmon, cook slowly, stirring, until the eggs are soft-cooked.

# FLOUNDER WITH
# MUSSEL SAUCE

| | |
|---|---|
| 2 doz. mussels | 1/2 cup water |
| 3 eggs, beaten lightly | 1 cup corn meal |
| 2 tsp. salt | 1/8 tsp. pepper |
| 8 flounder fillet | 1/2 cup butter |
| 2 tbsp. butter | 1/2 cup chives, minced |

Scrub mussels then place on rack in large kettle. Add water, bring to a boil, cover, reduce heat and steam for 15 minutes. Remove mussels from shell and chop finely. Reserve 1/3 cup cooking water. Melt 2 tablespoons butter, saute chives and mussels, add mussel liquid. Keep warm over low heat until fillets are browned. Dip fillets in egg then in corn meal to form a light coating. Brown fillets on both sides in 1/2 cup butter. Salt and pepper to taste. Serve browned fillets on a large platter topped with mussel sauce.

✳

# FRIED RAINBOW TROUT

| | |
|---|---|
| 6 1/2 lb. trout | 3 eggs, lightly beaten |
| 2 cup corn meal | 1 tsp. salt |
| 3 tbsp. butter | 1/4 tsp. pepper |

Dip trout in beaten egg, then in mixture of corn meal, salt and pepper. Coat each fish with seasoned meal. Heat butter in fry pan and fry trout for 4 to 5 minutes on each side.

✳

# BROILED
# RAINBOW TROUT

6 1/2 lb. trout                    3 tbsp. butter
1/2 tsp. salt                      1/8 tsp. pepper
1/4 cup minced parsley

Rub each fish well with butter.  Broil for 4 to 5 minutes per side. Baste with the drippings, season with salt and pepper and top with minced parsley.

# STEAMED POMPANO
# WITH GRAPES

4 lbs. pompano                    1 lb. muscadine grapes
2 tbsp. butter                    1/2 tsp. salt
1/4 tsp. pepper

Place cleaned fish on large piece of aluminum foil in a baking pan. Rub inside and outside of fish with butter and stuff with halved, seeded grapes, sprinkle inside out with salt and pepper. Cover with a second large piece of aluminum foil and seal edges. Bake at 400 F. for 30 minutes. Loosen top piece of foil, baste with drippings, reseal and steam for 15 minutes. Baste once more before serving.

## CODFISH BALLS

*Don't confuse these with the storebought variety!*

2 3/4 lbs. fresh cod     1 quart potatoes, diced
2 cup water     2 tbsp. butter
2 tsp. salt     1/4 tsp. pepper

Combine ingredients and boil, covered for 25 minutes. Drain well and mash, roll into 2" balls and deep fry.

＊

## BAKED SEA BASS
## WITH CHESTNUTS

4 lbs. sea bass     1 cup mushrooms
2 tbsp. oil     1 cup chestnuts, chopped
1 scallion, sliced     1 clove garlic, minced
1 cup apples, grated     1 cup bread crumbs
2 cup shrimp, chopped     1 tsp. salt
1/4 tsp. pepper     3/4 cup apple cider

Sprinkle bass inside and out with salt. Saute onions, garlic, and mushrooms in oil until golden and combine with remaining ingredients except cider. Lay fish on large piece of aluminum foil and wrap leaving a small vent at the top for basting. Place wrapped fish in baking pan and bake at 350 F. for one hour basting frequently with the apple cider.

＊

# 157.
# SHRIMP AND OKRA STEW

1 lb. okra, sliced
1 bay leaf, crumbled
1 cup water
1/2 tsp. gumbo file

6 tomatoes, chopped
10 peppercorns
1 1/2 lbs. shrimp
1 tsp. salt

Place okra, tomatoes, bay leaf, peppercorns, salt and water in a large kettle and simmer, covered, for 20 minutes or until tomatoes have broken up and okra is tender. Add shrimp and gumbo file mixed with one tablespoon of water, simmer 10 minutes and serve.

# HUPA HALIBUT WITH EGGS

4 halibut fillet
1 small onion, chopped
1/8 tsp. pepper
1 cup seaweed

2 cups chicken broth
1/2 tsp. salt
6 juniper berries, crushed
3 eggs

Bring broth to a boil, add onion, salt, pepper, and juniper berries. Simmer 15 minutes. Add halibut cut in bite-sized pieces. Simmer 10 minutes, add seaweed and drizzle in lightly beaten eggs. Cook until eggs are set up.

The recipe above, as traditionally prepared, was cooked in watertight baskets or cedar boxes into which were dropped hot stones to make the water boil. The eggs used were sea bird eggs collected from nests built in coastal cliffs. Halibut was a particularly important food source for the Tlingits who made special halibut hooks with shafts carved with figures which had magical powers.

## SMOKED EEL STEW

1 1/2 lbs. smoked eel
4 yellow onions
1/8 tsp. pepper

4 potatoes
6 cups water
1 tsp. salt

Cut eel into two inch pieces, slice onions, cube potatoes and add to boiling water. Add salt and pepper and simmer for about 1 hour. Skim off excess fat and serve.

Eels were a favorite food among Eastern tribes. They were taken from rivers and used fresh as well as being smoked or dried for winter eating. They were broiled on sapling sticks or broiled into thick soups as in the recipe above.

❋

## CHIPPEWA DILL
## JELLIED EEL

3 lbs. eel
2 tbsp. coarse salt
2 1/2 cup water
1/4 cup white wine
2 wild onions, minced

10 peppercorns
2 tsp. salt
2 bay leaves
1/4 cup lemon juice
2 tbsp. fresh dill

Skin the eel by cutting around the neck behind the fins. Wrap the head in a piece of paper towel, pull skin back to towel using pliers. Slit eel open, remove entrails and cut eel into two inch pieces. Wash well under running water. Put in a single layer in a shallow pan. Sprinkle with coarse salt and pour in enough water to cover eel completely. Soak 10 minutes, drain and rinse well in running water. Place eel in fireproof casserole. Add remaining ingredients except lemon juice and bring to a boil over high heat. Reduce heat and simmer for 20 minutes. Remove from heat and stir in lemon juice. When thoroughly chilled, the liquid should form a soft jelly. Serve from casserole.

## RED SNAPPER
## WITH ORANGES

*2 lbs. red snapper*  
*1/2 parsley, chopped*  
*2 tbsp. butter*  
*1/8 tsp. pepper*  
*4 oranges, sliced*

Place fish in large baking pan, dot well with butter and sprinkle with parsley and pepper. Lay the orange slices over the fish. Bake at 400 F. for 20 minutes. Reduce heat to 350 F. and bake 20 minutes more or until fish flakes at the touch of a fork.

# 160.
# SPICY MARINADE
# FISH BAKE

| | |
|---|---|
| 3 large trout | 3 cloves garlic, mashed |
| 2 tsp. red chili powder | 3 tsp. salt |
| 2 tsp. oregano | 3 tsp. onion, minced |
| 1 cup lemon juice | |

Combine last six ingredients and mix thoroughly. Let stand 15 minutes. Marinate trout in mixture for at least 30 minutes on each side. Wrap trout in cheese cloth wetting cloth with any remaining marinade. Wrap in foil. Bake fish at 350 F. for 1 1/2 hours.

✳

# PEROK

| | |
|---|---|
| 2 cups flour | 1/2 cup butter |
| Pinch of salt | 1 tbsp. water (approximately) |

Make a pie crust by cutting salt and butter into flour mixture forms oatmeal size particles. Add enough water to ball up the dry flour. Cool Weel and roll into top and bottom crust. Place bottom crust in pie pan and fill with the following ingredients:

| | |
|---|---|
| 1/2 salmon | 4 cooked rutabagas, cubed |
| 4 onions, chopped | 2 cups cooked rice |
| 2 eggs, lightly beaten | salt and pepper to taste |

Mix ingredients, pat into pan, place top crust on and seal crusts together in 375 F. oven for 45 minutes.

## DULSE-SHELLFISH STEW

| | |
|---|---|
| 2 cup dulse | 5 lbs. periwinkles, mussels, clams, |
| 2 onions, chopped | crab legs, shrimp, |
| 1 cup celery, chopped | 2 cloves garlic, minced |
| 5 potatoes, cubed | 2 bay leaves |
| 10 cups water | 2 tsp. salt |

Sear dulse in skillet, set aside. Bring water to boil, add all ingredients except shellfish and dulse. Cook until nearly tender. Add shellfish and dulse. Cook 10 minutes. NOTE: Dulse is a pinkish - red seaweed which grows on submerged rocks and ledges. It is a mineral-rich sea plant which is still widely used by coastal tribes.

## OYSTER & SNAPPER
## STEW

| | |
|---|---|
| 2 tbsp. butter | 1 onion, chopped |
| 4 cups chicken bouillon | 12-16 small new potatoes |
| 1 medium green apple | 1 tbsp. lemon juice |
| 3-4 lbs. red snapper | 24 oysters (about 2 cups) |
| 2 cups milk | 1/2 tsp. celery seed |
| | 1 tbsp. fresh tarragon |

Melt butter in large pan, saute onion until translucent, add boullion and potatoes. Raise heat to high and cook about seven minutes until potatoes are done. Cut apple into 1/4 inch julienne sticks and toss with lemon juice to prevent discoloring. Set aside. Add snapper cut in 2" cubes to soup, lower heat and simmer 10 minutes until done. Add oysters, and milk and bring to a boil. Immediately remove from heat, add celery seeds. Serve sprinkled with apple sticks.

## SCALLOPS WITH

## GINGER & MINT

| | |
|---|---|
| 4 tbsp. butter | 2 carrots, finely grated |
| 5 scallions, sliced | 1 tbsp. ginger, minced |
| 1/2 tsp. salt | 1/4 tsp. pepper |
| 2 lbs. small bay scallops | 2 tbsp. mint, chopped |

Saute ginger and scallions in butter until tender. Add scallops a few at a time cooking approximately 2 minutes per batch. Set aside. Add carrots, stir, cover and cook until softened (about 15 minutes). Add scallops and mint, remove immediately from heat once scallops are warmed through.

## BROILED SHRIMP

| | |
|---|---|
| 4 1/2 lbs. shrimp | 1 3/4 cup water |
| 4 cloves garlic, crushed | 1/2 cup oil |
| 1/4 tsp. oregano | 2 tsp. salt |
| 1/4 tsp. pepper | |

Place shrimp in large kettle, add 1 tsp. salt. Steam shrimp for 20 minutes and drain reserving one cup of broth. Mix garlic, oil, oregano, pepper, and remaining salt. Shell and devein shrimp. Place on broiler pan, pour garlic mixture over shrimp and broil for 5 minutes. Turn shrimp, pour shrimp broth over them and broil 2 minutes longer, basting with broth. Top each serving with a little of the broth.

# SHELLFISH BAKE

*Seaweed*                                        *Assorted shellfish*

Dig a pit 4 feet square and 4 feet deep. Line the pit with stones and build a large fire and keep hot for four hours. Brush coals aside and cover rocks with a 4 inch layer of seaweed. Lay shellfish—clams, mussels, periwinkles, sea urchins and crab—on seaweed layer. Cover seafood with 6 inch layer of seaweed. Lay branches or brush on seaweed to hold in steam. The shellfish should be cooked in about an hour but can be left as long as 2 hours before eating.

NOTE:  A slight variation on the shellfish bake was used by the Klallam tribe.  Upon finding a limpet covered rock, they covered it with seaweed which they heaped with hot stones. The limpets loosened their hold on the rock as they cooked and were either eaten on the spot or scraped off and taken home.

✳

# PAN FRIED PERCH

*4 perch - more if small*                        *salt and pepper*
*flour*                        *butter and shortening (equal amounts)*

Shake fish in a bag with flour, salt and pepper, coating thoroughly. Melt butter and shortening in a skillet. Cook fish over a bush fire until brown on both sides. Serve while crisp and hot with butter or tartar sauce.

# BASS FILLETS AND STUFFED OLIVES

6 bass fillets
salt and pepper
1/2 cup dry white wine
3 tbsp. oil
2 onions, sliced

1 tbsp. pimento, chopped
2 ripe tomatoes, sliced
1 tbsp. vinegar
1 tsp. salt
parsley

12 stuffed olives

Arrange fillets in buttered baking dish and season with salt and pepper. Pour the wine around the fillets.

Heat oil in skillet; add onions and simmer for 5 minutes. Add olives, pimento, tomatoes, vinegar and salt. Simmer for 20 minutes longer. Spread the sauce over the fillets and bake at 350 F for 30 minutes. When ready to serve, sprinkle with parsley.

✳

# FRESH BASS SOUP

3 slices boiled salt pork
2 lbs. bass, filleted
1 large onion, sliced thin

1 1/2 cups hot milk
1 tsp. savory
2 tbsp. butter or margarine

2 cups sliced potatoes

Cut salt pork into 1 1/2 inch squares and brown in a skillet. Cut fish into 1 inch pieces. Making alternate layers of potatoes, onions and fish in a baking dish. Add salt pork and cover with water and bring to a boil. Reduce heat and simmer for 15 minutes, or until potatoes are tender. Add milk, savory and butter. Do not mix, simply keep warm until ready to serve.

# CARP IN BEER

| | |
|---|---|
| **4 lbs. carp fillets,** | **1 lemon, sliced** |
| **cut into serving pieces** | **1 tbsp. flour** |
| **salt** | **1 tbsp. butter** |
| **3 cups of beer** | **1 tbsp. sugar** |
| **2 onions, sliced** | **1 bay leaf** |
| **6 peppercorns** | |

Sprinkle fish with salt and let it sit for 1/2 hour. Place fish in a saucepan. Pour in beer and add onions, bay leaf, peppercorns, and lemon. Simmer until fish is tender about 30 to 45 minutes. Remove fish to platter. Make a paste of flour and butter and stir into broth. Add sugar and simmer until hot. Pour the sauce over fish. Serve.

✳

# CATFISH BAKE

| | |
|---|---|
| **6 or 7 catfish, skinned and cleaned** | **1/8 tsp. tarragon** |
| **3 tbsp. butter or margarine** | **1/4 tsp. marjoram** |
| **1 cup evaporated milk** | **1/2 cup flour** |
| **1/2 tsp. dry mustard** | |

Melt butter in a baking dish. Mix flour with mustard tarragon, and marjoram. Dip fish in milk, then roll in flour mixture and lay them in hot butter. Bake at 325 F for 15 to 20 minutes. Remove from oven and turn fish over. Place back in the oven for another 15 to 20 minutes. Serve on a hot platter.

## SKILLET FRIED
## CATFISH

6 catfish, skinned and cleaned          1/2 cup canned milk
8 tbsp. bacon fat                       1/2 tsp. salt
1/2 cup cornmeal                        1/4 tsp. pepper

Sprinkle the inside of the fish with salt and pepper. Dip fish, first in milk, then into cornmeal. Melt bacon fat in a heavy skillet and fry fish until golden brown on one side, about 4 to 5 minutes. Turn carefully and fry the other side, until fish flakes easily when tested with a fork. Serve with favorite sauce.

※

## CATFISH DELIGHT

8 catfish
prepared mustard
1 cup flour
bacon fat

Fillet fish and wash in cold water. Pat dry. Spread mustard on both sides of the fillets. Dredge with flour and fry in hot bacon fat until golden brown.

## CATFISH STEW

2 slices bacon
1 large onion, chopped
1 large can tomatoes
2 large potatoes, diced
1 tsp. salt

1 cup boiling water
2 tbsp. worcestershire sauce
1/4 cup catsup
1/4 tsp. thyme
1 1/2 lbs. skinned catfish

In a heavy saucepan or dutch oven, fry onions with chopped bacon. Then add tomatoes, water, and other ingredients, except fish. Cover and simmer for 30 minutes. Add bite size pieces of fish and cook for 15 minutes uncovered.

## CASSEROLE

## OF EELS

3 lbs. eel
salted water
1/2 cup flour
1 tsp. salt
1/8 tsp. pepper

1/4 cup butter
12 small peeled onions
1 bay leaf
2 cups water
1 cup mushrooms

Skin and clean the eel thoroughly and cut into 3 inch pieces. Soak in cold salted water for 1 hour. Drain and pat dry. Sprinkle with salt and pepper. Then brown in melted butter. Put eel in a casserole dish and add onions, bay leaf and water. Cover and bake at 350 F for 35 minutes. Add mushrooms and cook for another 25 minutes.

# MUSKELLUNGE

1 muskellunge, filleted
salt and pepper to taste
garlic powder

1 cup pancake mix
water
fat for frying

onion powder

Cut the muskie fillets into serving pieces. Using commercial pancake mix add enough water to make a batter. Mix salt, pepper, garlic and onion into the batter. Heat oil in a wok. Dip fish in batter and then place in wok. Turn once and cook until both sides are a deep golden brown. Serve.

✳

# MUSKIE STEAKS

1 muskellunge, dressed
salt and pepper to taste
Italian salad dressing
butter, melted

Cut muskie into thin steaks. Make marinade by combining salt, pepper and Italian salad dressing. Marinate the steaks for a few hours turning once after 1 hour. Lightly grease a shallow broiling pan. Place steaks on the broiler and broil until golden brown on each side. Baste with a combination of melted butter and marinade. Place on platter and pour remaining butter and marinade over them. Serve.

## BAKED MUSKELLUNGE

| | |
|---|---|
| *1 muskellunge, filleted* | *cheese, grated* |
| *butter, melted* | *salt and pepper to taste* |
| *onion, chopped finely* | *garlic powder* |
| *lemon juice* | |

Line a baking dish with foil leaving enough foil to fold over and seal in the fish. Cut fillets into serving size pieces and season with salt, pepper and garlic. Brush foil with 1/2 the butter and 1/2 the lemon and place fish in dish. Sprinkle onion over the fish and pour remaining butter and lemon juice over top. Fold over the foil and bake at 350 F for 45 minutes. Peel back foil and sprinkle with grated cheese. Put back in oven just until cheese melts. Serve.

## PICKEREL N' SAUCE

| | |
|---|---|
| *1 lb. pickerel, serving pieces* | *flour* |
| *1 medium onion, diced* | *1/2 tsp. pepper* |
| *1 can mushroom soup* | *1 tsp. salt* |
| *1/2 cup milk* | *2 tbsp. bacon drippings* |

Wash and pat dry fillets; then dredge with flour. Sprinkle on salt and pepper. In a skillet, melt bacon drippings, then add fillets to brown on all sides. Add onion, mushroom soup and milk; cover and cook over medium heat for 30 minutes.

## PICKEREL BISQUE

fish to serve 4
4 cups fish stock
sprig of thyme
3 tbsp. butter

1 cup heavy cream
1/4 tsp. parsley
salt and pepper
crumbled crackers

1 tbsp. flour

Fillet the fish.  Make a fish stock, using heads, tails and bones. Strain stock, add fillets, and simmer until they flake.  Remove fish and chop fine.  In a saucepan, melt butter, stir in the flour until smooth.  Stir in the stock and bring to a boil, then add fish, cream, parsley, salt and pepper to taste.  Heat thoroughly, pour over the crackers and serve.

✹

## PICKEREL SOUP

2 lbs. filleted pickerel
2 tbsp. butter or margarine
2 tbsp. cooking oil
1 large onion, minced
1 large carrot, grated
2 tomatoes, peeled and sliced

1/4 tsp. thyme
1/4 tsp. savory
1 tsp. salt
1/2 tsp. pepper
2 quarts boiling water
1 cup uncooked noodles

Cut fish into serving pieces.  Put butter, oil, carrots, onions, and tomatoes in large pan and simmer for 10 minutes.  Add water and noodles. Bring to a boil, then reduce heat and add thyme, savory, salt and pepper.  Carefully add fish and simmer for 20 minutes.

## PIKEBURGER

| | |
|---|---|
| 1 1/2 to 2 lbs. ground pike | 1 tsp. lemon juice |
| 1 onion, chopped fine | 1/4 tsp. pepper |
| 1 egg | 1 cup bread crumbs |
| 1/2 tsp. salt | bacon fat |

pinch each of tarragon, thyme and parsley

Combine egg, salt, pepper and seasonings. Mix in pike, onion, lemon juice and bread crumbs. Shape into patties and fry in bacon fat as you would hamburger.

✳

## BROILED OPEN PIKE

| | |
|---|---|
| 1 pike | 1 tbsp. lemon juice |
| butter | 1 tbsp. flour |
| salt and pepper | 1 cup dry white wine |

1 tsp. water

Split fish lengthwise. Place fish in a buttered broiler pan, skin side down. Sprinkle with salt and pepper. Baste fish with lemon juice and butter and place under broiler, about 6 inches away from heat. Baste frequently with wine and lemon juice mixture. Fish is done when it flakes easily with a fork.

## PIKE CASSEROLE

2 lbs. filleted pike, cut in pieces     salt and pepper to taste
4 large potatoes, peeled and sliced     1 large onion, chopped
4 slices bacon, chopped

Lightly grease baking dish and alternate layers of fish, onion and potatoes, beginning and ending with potatoes. Distribute chopped bacon over each layer. Sprinkle with salt and pepper. Cover the mixture with cold water. Cover and bake at 350 F for 35 to 40 minutes.

✳

## SALMON LOAVES

2 cups boiled salmon     1/2 tsp. baking powder
3 eggs, beaten     1/4 tsp. pepper
1/2 cup bread crumbs     2 tbsp. lemon juice
4 tbsp. melted butter     1 tbsp. parsley, chopped
1/2 cup cream     1 tsp. lemon rind, grated

Mix all ingredients together, blending very well. Pour mixture into a greased loaf pan. Bake at 350 F for 30 minutes.

# SALMON RICE SALAD

| | |
|---|---|
| 1 1/2 cups cooked rice | 1 tsp. horseradish sauce |
| 1/4 cup french dressing | 1/2 tsp. celery salt |
| 3/4 cup mayonnaise | 1/2 tsp. celery, chopped |
| 1/2 tsp. salt | 1 hard boiled egg, diced |
| 1/4 tsp. pepper | 1/2 cucumber, peeled and sliced |
| 1 tbsp. onion, finely chopped | 1 cup cooked salmon |

While rice is still hot, add french dressing. Cool to room temperature before adding remaining ingredients. Mix lightly. Chill for 1 hour before serving.

# MACARONI
# SALMON CASSEROLE

| | |
|---|---|
| margarine | salt and pepper to taste |
| 2 cups cooked salmon | 1 (10 oz.) can mushroom or celery soup |
| 4 cups macaroni, cooked | 1/2 cup water or milk |
| 1 medium onion, chopped | 1 cup cracker crumbs |

In a casserole dish, combine the salmon, macaroni, onion, salt and pepper. Mix in the soup and the milk or water. Sprinkle the top with the cracker crumbs and dot with margarine. Bake at 350 F for 45 minutes.

# CHAPTER FIVE

# ·CLEANING, SKINNING & TANNING OF FISH AND GAME·

Before any recipe can begin, the cleaning and skinning process must be completed.

On the following pages you will find the necessary information needed to clean, skin, and tan the various animals mentioned in our recipes as well as cleaning and preparation guides for fowl and fish.

## BIG GAME ANIMALS

Instructions for deer and other big game animals

Quick cleaning and cooling is of the utmost importance. First of all, lay the deer with its head downhill and cut the throat so that it will bleed thoroughly. Lay the deer flat on its back and slit the belly all the way down to within 6 inches of its tail, being careful not to cut the intestine. Make a circular cut completely around the vent to free it and the large intestine. Cut the windpipe. Then cut the diaphragm which separates the chest from the abdominal cavity. Now grab the front legs, jerking and rolling the deer over, the insides will spill out on the ground. Cut out the heart and the liver and save. Do all this quickly and thoroughly. In case of punctured organs, there will be bleeding which causes contamination.

The carcass should be cooled quickly. If the weather prevents this, rub the inside with black pepper. This will keep the flies away. Prop the carcass open with a stick so that the air will circulate. If there is a part of the meat which has been badly shot up, it should be cut away. If its condition isn't too bad you can soak it overnight in a brine to remove the blood and then use it for venison burgers.

When you skin the deer, hang it up by the hind feet and cut the hide around the ankles. Make cuts from the inner thighs to the vent. Pull the skin down. It may be so firmly adhered that you will need to use a knife to loosen it.

## SKINNING AND FILLETING FISH

Make a cut along the dorsal fins, the lower edge of the belly and just behind the gills. Holding the head of the fish with the left hand, take the upper left corner of the skin in a pair of pliers and pull it towards you. Repeat this on the other side, then remove head and entrails. Wash fish thoroughly inside and out with cold water. You will find that blood clings to the backbone but can be removed by scrubbing with a small brush. Shake salt inside the cavity along the backbone. A few small gashes along the backbone will prevent the fish from curling in the skillet.

## HOW TO FILLET A FISH

Cut through the skin from the head to tail along the backbone on each side of the dorsal fin. Cut a V-shaped notch behind the head, cutting to the backbone. Cut through the skin and pull it towards the tail, holding the fish in your hand. Cut to the backbone. Turn the knife to a horizontal position and slide it along the backbone, cutting off the flesh in one slab. Turn the fish, and repeat on the other side. If the fish tends to slip away from you, you can nail the head to a board. Check the fillet for any bones and wash thoroughly with cold water.

## SKINNING AND DRESSING OF
## SMALL GAME ANIMALS

### BEAVER

Lay beaver on its back and cut off legs at the first joints. Cut pelt in a straight line down the chest and belly to vent. Pull skin from flesh, being careful when you pull legs through the skin. Cut off tail and head.

Make a cut through the layer of meat from the breast bone to the vent, encircling the vent. Lay body cavity open and remove the entrails. Carefully cut out tiny musk glands from under the skin on the inside of legs, and be sure to remove the castor gland under the belly near the tail. Trim off all fat. Wash and soak meat with warm salted water

BEAVER TAILS : Wash thoroughly. roast until skin begins to blister. Remove; cool; peel skin off. You may now roast or boil in salted water until tender.

### FROG LEGS

Cut the legs from the frog. Wash them, and peel the skin back so it will come off rather like a glove. Cut off the feet. Pour boiling water over the legs, drain and dry them. They are now ready to cook.

### GROUND HOG

Dress ground hog as you would a beaver, but watch for and remove 7 to 9 small sacs or kernels in the small of the back and under the forepaws. Wash and soak carcass with warm salted water.

### MUSKRAT

Slit skin on the inside of the hind legs, from the paws to the vent and cut off both hind and forepaws and tail. Then work skin off inside out. Remove head from the carcass. Insert knife at the tip of breastbone and slit muskrat down the front. Open body cavity and remove the entrails. Cut out musk glands from inside the legs, plus white tissuey skin, and all fat. Wash and soak meat with warm salted water.

**MUSKRAT TAILS:** Cut off the tails and dip them into very hot water. Pull off the fur. One can either cook them on the top of the stove, turning them after a few minutes, or boil them. Muskrat and beaver tails are very sticky to eat.

### RACCOON

Skin by cutting around the hind legs and the inside of the thigh to the crotch. Loosen the skin and work towards head. When you have reached the head, you can cut off the head and feet. Cut a slit down the belly and remove the entrails. Wash and soak in warm salted water.

### PORCUPINE

To ready the porcupine for cleaning, first remove quills by burning them off, then scrape right down to the hide. This method adds to the flavor of the meat. Otherwise, skinning process is the same as that of raccoon. The porcupine is at its best when trapped and cooked in September.

### RABBIT

To dress rabbit, cut front legs at the first joint. Cut through skin around hind legs. Tie hind legs together and hang rabbit. Pull skin down off the hind legs and peel it off, inside out over the body and forelegs. Cut head off. Slit rabbit down the front and remove the entrails. Wash meat with warm water.

### TURTLE

Remove the head from the turtle and hang the shell neck down on a hook for 1/2 hour until the blood stops dripping. Then wash the turtle and drop it into boiling water and cook for 10 minutes. Pour off the water and cover the turtle with cold water. Let it stand until cool enough to handle. Rub the nails and black skin from the legs with a towel.

Wash the turtle carefully and place it in a pot. Cover it with boiling water and simmer; cover until the flesh is tender. This will be when the joints of the legs can be broken with slight pressure and the shell easily separates. This will take 50 to 60 minutes. Remove the turtle from the water, cool and place turtle on its back with the head end away from you. Loosen and remove the under shell. The liver, gall bladder and sand bag will be found near the head end, the gall being attached to the left side of the liver. Take out the gall as you would that of a chicken, being careful not to break it. Remove the entrails and throw them away. Then take out the eggs, if any. Remove the slight membrane and drop the eggs in cold water. Cut up the meat very fine.

## DRESSING OF GAME BIRDS

If you are not able to pluck your bird in the field, at least clean it as much as possible. Cut the throat and hang the head down to bleed. Remove the feathers from the crop and tail, pulling them gently towards the tail so as to not break the skin. Slit the skin up over the crop and remove it. Cut down to the vent and remove the entrails, separating the giblets and putting them back in the cavity or in a separate bag. Carefully cut away the oil sac at the base of the tail.

It is much easier to pluck a bird that is thoroughly chilled. To pluck, pick all pin feathers from a bird. After removing the coarser feathers, if those remaining are downy or small, you may use the paraffin method. Make a mixture of two gallons of boiling water with 1/2 pound of melted paraffin wax. Dip the duck so it becomes coated with wax, it will take several dips to build up a sufficiently thick coat. Let the paraffin wax cool and harden. You may scrape it off with a dull knife or you may roll it off with your fingers.

It may be advisable to skin the bird, if the skin has been badly torn by shooting. Cut through the skin over the breast, peeling the remainder of the skin and feathers from the bird.

# TANNING FURS AND LEATHERS

| ANIMAL | USE | CHARACTERISTICS |
|--------|-----|-----------------|
| Bear | rugs | hard, durable |
| Beaver | coats | wears well |
| Deer | gloves, coats moccasins | soft, pliable, wears very well |
| Muskrat | coats | wears well |
| Rabbit | gloves | fairly delicate |
| Raccoon | hats, coats | wears well |
| Squirrel | coats | delicate fur |
| Ground Hog | gloves | delicate fur |

## EQUIPMENT AND SUPPLIES

Skinning knife - to remove hide
(regular knife may be used but it must be razor sharp).
Rubber gloves
Plastic and wooden containers
Wooden stir stick
Neat's foot oil or corn oil
Salt or borax
Fleshing knife, butcher knife or draw knife
Hydrated lime (needed for dehairing)
Alum
Oatmeal or hardwood sawdust
Sandpaper

# STEP BY STEP
# TANNING INSTRUCTIONS

1. Remove the hide from the animal being careful neither to cut through the skin nor to leave big chunks of flesh on the animal.

2 a) Fleshing occurs once the hide has been removed from the animal. This process involves removing bits of meat and fat that are still on the hide. To make the job easier first soak the skin in a solution of either salt or borax using the following proportions.

**1 pound salt per 2 gallons of soft water**
**1 ounce borax per gallon of water**

(NOTE - Use hot water to dissolve the borax but let it cool off before immersing the skin). An agitator type washing machine will speed up the soaking process and also help reduce hair loss by avoiding over-soaking. Soak for about 12 hours or overnight. Remove from solution and rinse in fresh water and let drain. While the flesh side is still moist, rub in the salt until the flesh side is completely covered (avoid getting salt into the fur side.).

When the first application has soaked in, apply second. Fold the hide in half lengthwise, flesh side to flesh side; then roll it up and place on a slanted surface so that it can drain.

Begin fleshing the next day. Place the hide fur side down on a smooth log and scrape away the fat and gristle with a fleshing knife, butcher knife, or a drawknife. Scrape carefully and evenly. The membrane on the hides inner surface must be removed for tanning to be successful. Scrape with the blunt edge occasionally to help soften the leather. After fleshing is complete, wash the hide in a soapy solution, then rinse quickly and thoroughly.

b) **De-hairing** - If you wish to remove the hair, it is necessary to soak the hide in a de-hairing solution. Use 1 pound of hydrated lime per 8 gallons of soft water and soak for about 5 days, stirring twice a day or longer if the weather is cold, in a wooden or plastic container (lime is caustic). When the hair is loose, rinse the hide then place it's fur side up on a smooth log and scrape off the hair and loose surface skin with the dull edge of your fleshing knife. When all the hair is removed then proceed to tan.

3. **Tanning** - This solution has certain advantages over some other methods:

1) The hide will not overtan.
2) It has no dangerous acids or toxic vapors.

It is still necessary to use rubber gloves. In a large plastic or wooden container, add 5 pounds of salt to 10 gallons of warm soft water (rain water will do). Next mix 2 pounds alum in enough hot water to dissolve it. Mix the 2 solutions together, stirring with a wooden paddle until the ingredients are thoroughly mixed. The solution can be used warm or cold but not hot. Immerse the hide in the tanning solution and stir gently about twice a day.

Make certain the solution reaches every nook and cranny in the hide, the larger the hide the longer it takes to tan. A rabbit takes about 2 days and a deer takes about 7 days. To test for complete tanning cut off a little bit of the hide and if the color is uniform all the way through, the hide is tanned. It is very important to tan completely.

4. When the hide is tanned, remove it from the solution and rinse it either with a garden hose or in a sink with many changes of water.

5. Next hang it over something out of direct sunlight and in such a way that the air can circulate around the hide.

6. After several days while the hair and hide are still damp, fold the hide flesh side to flesh side and roll it up. Leave it like this overnight.

If the hide has dried before you were able to roll it up use a wet sponge to dampen the flesh side before you roll it up.

7. Work the hide by stretching and pulling it over a smooth surface, continue in this manner until the hide is pliable.

8. When the hide is pliable, with the tips of your fingers, rub in neat's foot or corn oil on the flesh side. Use warm oil.

9. To clean the fur side, fill a plastic bag with oatmeal or hardwood sawdust and shake until fur is clean.

10. Brush and comb fur until it is entirely fluffed up. Use coarse sandpaper on any rough spots on flesh side.

### THE HIDE IS NOW READY TO USE

✳

# CHAPTER SIX

## · WILD RICE ·

Wild rice ripens in August. It usually grows in moving waters about 3 to 4 feet deep. The very long seed-like grass is often 8 to 10 feet tall and has a long brown-like flower on top. To harvest, bind the plant over your canoe and beat the pulp, causing the fruit to fall into the canoe.

To preserve wild rice, first spread out in a warm place until it is thoroughly dried. Then, bake in a shallow pan for about two hours at 225 F., stirring occasionally to parch it evenly.

After drying, the husk can be loosened by pounding and rubbing through the hands. Store in jars and seal. Always wash the rice thoroughly before using, otherwise it has disagreeable smoky flavor.

## BAKED WILD RICE

1/2 medium onion, minced    2 cups homemade chicken stock
1/4 cup butter    2 tbsp. butter
1 cup wild rice    salt

Saute onion in a dutch oven. Add rice and stir until well mixed. Bring chicken stock to a boil in a saucepan. Add broth to rice. Cover tightly and bake for 25 minutes. Mix rice gently with 2 tablespoons of butter and salt. Serve.

✳

## WILD RICE
## SPOON BREAD

1 cup cooked wild rice    1 tsp. salt
1/4 cup corn meal    2 eggs, beaten
2 cups buttermilk    2 tbsp. melted butter
1/2 tsp. baking soda

Combine above ingredients together one at a time in order given. Put batter in a greased baking dish and bake at 325 F for 1 hour.

✳

## QUICK WILD

## RICE DISH

2 cups wild rice (cooked)
1/2 cup onion, chopped
1/4 lb. mushrooms, sliced
1/4 cup chopped almonds
2 tbsp. butter

1 tbsp. flour
1/2 cup beef bouillon
1/2 tsp. salt
1/2 tsp. pepper
1/2 cup chopped parsley

Drain rice. Saute onions and mushrooms in butter. Stir in flour. Add bouillon and simmer, stirring frequently till smooth. Add seasonings, wild rice and almonds. Serve.

## SPEEDY WILD

## RICE PUDDING

1 package instant vanilla pudding
(4 serving package)
2 cups milk
dash nutmeg

1 1/2 cups wild rice, cooked
1/4 cup raisins, cooked

Prepare pudding as directed with milk adding nutmeg. Mix in cooled rice and raisins. Chill for 15 minutes before serving.

## STIR FRIED WILD
## RICE 'N VEGETABLES

1/2 cup wild rice
3 tbsp. vegetable oil
4 green onions, sliced
2 tbsp. soya sauce
1/4 tsp. pepper

1 1/2 cups boiling water
1 clove garlic, sliced
1 cup of bean sprouts
1/4 tsp. ginger
2 cups spinach leaves

Prepare wild rice, next, stir in rice to 1 1/2 cups boiling water. Simmer for 25 minutes, covered. Drain. Saute garlic in oil for 5 minutes. Remove garlic. Stir fry onions and celery in oil (5 min). Add bean sprouts, cooked wild rice, soya sauce, ginger and pepper. Stir fry for 5 minutes. Add spinach leaves and stir fry for 2 min.

✳

## CHIPPEWA
## WILD RICE

1 cup wild rice, washed in cold water
2 1/2 cups water
1 1/2 tsp. salt

1/4 tsp. pepper
2 tbsp. minced chives
bacon drippings plus melted butter
or 4 strips bacon cut into julienne strips
margarine to measure 1/3 cup
6 eggs

Place the wild rice, water and 1 tsp. salt in a saucepan, and bring slowly to a boil. Reduce heat and simmer uncovered until all water is absorbed. Render the bacon in a large heavy skillet. Drain bacon on paper towelling. Save drippings. Beat eggs , 1/2 tsp. salt and the pepper until light. Pour into the skillet in which you browned the bacon, and brown the eggs lightly. Then turn gently, as you would a pancake, and brown on the other side. When eggs are firm, cut into julienne strips. Lightly toss the bacon, julienne egg strips, chives, bacon drippings plus melted butter or margarine with the rice. Serve hot as a main dish.

# BAKED WILD RICE

# AND CARROTS

*1 1/2 cups wild rice, washed in cold water*
*4 mushrooms, chopped*

*2 1/2 cups water*                     *4 slices bacon, cut into strips*
*2 1/2 tsp. salt*                        *1 cup finely grated carrots*
*1 onion, peeled and chopped*              *1/2 cup light cream*
*1 egg*

Place the wild rice, water, salt in a large saucepan, and bring to a boil. Boil vigorously for about 10 minutes. Turn off heat, cover, and let rice stand for about 20 minutes or until all the water has been absorbed. Brown the bacon, remove from drippings, and drain on paper towelling. Saute the onions and mushrooms in the bacon drippings until the onions are golden and transparent. Mix the bacon, sauted onions and mushrooms, and grated carrots into the wild rice. Beat the cream and eggs until light, and fold into the wild rice mixture. Bake, covered, in a buttered 1 1/2 quart casserole in a moderately slow oven, 325 F., for 30 minutes. Remove cover, stir the mixture well with a fork, bake for 15 minutes at the same temperature. Stir once again and bake, uncovered, for 15 minutes longer.

# · CHAPTER SEVEN ·
# SAUCES, MARINADES, STUFFINGS, BATTERS AND BREADS

## THIN CREAMY SAUCE

*1 cup milk*
*1 tablespoon flour*
*1 tablespoon fat*
*1/2 teaspoon seasoning*

Excellent for creamy soup base .

✳

## MEDIUM WHITE SAUCE

*1 cup milk*
*2 tablespoons flour*
*1 1/2 tablespoon fat*
*1/2 tablespoon seasoning*

Use this sauce for creamed and scalloped dishes or as a gravy.

✳

# TASTY SOUFFLE SAUCE

*1 cup milk*
*3 tablespoons flour*
*2 tablespoons fat*
*1 teaspoon seasoning*

This sauce, and a wise selection of seasoning for the particular dish, is wonderful for various souffles.

# THICK CROQUETTE

# WHITE SAUCE

*1 cup milk*
*4 tablespoons flour*
*2 1/2 tablespoons fat*
*1 teaspoon seasoning*

# MOOSE MARINADE

1 cup pineapple juice
1/2 cup honey
1/2 tsp. allspice

Combine above ingredients and brush on meat. Fry or roast. The longer meat is left to marinate the better it will taste.

# VENISON MARINADE

1/2 cup salad oil
1/4 cup vinegar
1/4 cup onion, chopped
1 tsp. salt
2 tsp. worcestershire sauce

Combine all above ingredients. Let meat stand in marinade for 2 hours at room temperature.
If marinade does not fully cover meat, turn meat several times.

## SPICY VENISON
## MARINADE

One part vinegar or lemon juice with 3 parts salad or olive oil.
Season with your preference of spices and items from the following list:

| | |
|---|---|
| 1/4 tsp. dill seed | 2 medium sliced onions |
| 1/4 tsp. celery seed | 1 clove garlic, crushed |
| 1/4 tsp. cloves | 1/2 tsp. celery flakes |
| 1 -2 bay leaves | 1 tsp. parsley flakes |
| 2 sliced carrots | |

NOTE: When marinating meat, cover meat entirely or turn several times and then refrigerate from 4 to 12 hours.

＊

## BARBECUE SAUCE

| | |
|---|---|
| 1 medium onion, chopped | 2 tbsp. vinegar |
| 1 garlic clove, minced | 1 tbsp. brown sugar |
| 2 tbsp. margarine or butter | 1 tsp. salt |
| 1/2 cup catsup | 1 tsp. dry mustard |
| 1/4 cup water | 1/2 tsp. tabasco sauce |

Saute onion and garlic in butter or margarine until tender. Add remaining ingredients and bring to a boil. Brush on roasts, ribs or steaks.

## VENISON STEAK
## CHASEUR (SAUCE)

*2 tbsp. butter*           *2 tsp. wine or cider vinegar*
*2 tbsp. flour*            *1 tsp. grape or currant jelly*
*3/4 cup consomme*         *1/2 tsp. salt*
*3 tsp. tomato paste*      *1/4 tsp. pepper*

Melt butter.  Add flour and stir over low heat until lightly browned.  Add tomato paste and consomme, then stir until smooth and creamy. Cook over low heat for 1 hour stirring once or twice. Add vinegar, jelly, salt and pepper.

✳

## EGG SAUCE
## FOR FISH

*2 tbsp. margarine or butter*              *1 cup milk*
*1 tbsp. flour*            *3 hard boiled eggs, sliced finely*

Melt margarine in a saucepan and mix in flour until well blended. Slowly mix in milk and bring to a boil.  Stir in eggs and remove pan from heat.  Pour sauce over fish and serve.

## MUSHROOM SAUCE

1 - 1 1/2 cups mushrooms, sliced          2 cups of beef bouillon
4 tbsp. margarine                        1/3 cup of all purpose flour
1 small onion, minced                    1/2 tsp. each of salt and pepper
1 garlic clove

Melt margarine in a saucepan and saute onion, mushrooms and garlic. Add beef bouillon and increase heat to medium for 10 minutes. Combine flour, salt, and pepper. Add mixture to saucepan and gently boil for 5 minutes. Pour heated sauce over meat.

✳

## HOT SAUCE

2 medium onions, sliced          3 1/2 cups tomato juice
1 clove garlic, chopped fine     1/4 tsp. worcestershire sauce
1 tbsp. chopped parsley          salt and pepper to taste
3 tbsp. butter, margarine or oil

Cook onions, garlic and parsley in fat until onion is golden brown. Add tomato juice and worcestershire sauce and cook gently for 15 minutes. Season with salt and pepper.

## GWAP GIZ GUN

*2 cups flour*
*2 tbsp. baking powder*
*1/2 tsp. salt*
*1/2 cup water or buttermilk*

Combine first three ingredients; then make a well and mix in liquid. Turn out on floured board and knead. Flatten with palm of hand and roll out to 1/2 inch in thickness. Place on back of a woodstove that has been sprinkled with salt. Cook until light brown on one side, then turn over. Do not have stove too hot. When cooked, spread with margarine and sprinkle with salt.

❋

## SHUSWAP BANNOCK

*3 cups all purpose flour*            *1 1/2 cups water*
*1 tbsp. baking powder*               *1 cup blueberries*
*1 1/2 tsp. salt*

Mix dry ingredients together, then add water quickly and continue to stir. Spread on a pie plate and put in oven at 425 F for 20 minutes.

## BACON CORNBREAD

| | |
|---|---|
| 1 1/3 cups flour | 1 egg, beaten |
| 1 cup cornmeal | 1 1/2 cups evaporated milk |
| 1/2 cup sugar | 4 tsp. vinegar |
| 1 1/2 tsp. baking powder | 1/3 cup melted butter |
| 1/2 tsp. baking soda | bacon drippings |
| 1 tsp. salt | 8 slices cooked bacon, crumbled |

Combine flour, cornmeal, sugar, baking powder, baking soda, salt and crumbled bacon. In a separate bowl combine egg, evaporated milk and bacon drippings. Add to flour mixture and stir just until moistened. Pour into greased 8 inch square pan. Bake at 350 F for 40 to 45 minutes.

To Serve: Serve warm with maple syrup

## GRANDMA'S SWEET BISCUITS

| | |
|---|---|
| 3 cups flour | 1/2 cup raisins |
| 2 tbsp. baking powder | 1/2 lb. lard |
| 1/2 tsp. salt | 1/2 cup water |

1 cup brown sugar

Combine first four ingredients, then add raisins. Cut lard into flour mixture and stir. Make a well in center slowly mix in water. Use only enough water to hold dough together. Shape dough into a ball; then turn out onto a floured board. Knead 3 to 4 times, then roll out to 1/2 inch thickness. Cut with a round cutter and bake at 375 F for 35 to 40 minutes.

## POTATO SCONES

2 cups flour

1 tsp. salt

3 tsp. baking powder

1 tbsp. shortening

1 cup cold mashed potatoes

1 egg

1/3 cup milk

Mix together flour, salt and baking powder. Mix in shortening and cold potatoes. Beat egg and stir in milk. Add to potato mixture. Roll 3/8 inch thick on a floured board and cut into squares. Cook slowly in greased frying pan. Turn several times so that cakes brown on both sides.

## FRIED BREAD

5 cups all purpose flour

10 tsp. baking powder

4 tbsp. sugar

2 tbsp. vegetable oil

2 eggs, beaten

2 cups water

1/2 tsp. salt

Sift together flour, baking powder, sugar and salt. In a separate bowl, combine vegetable oil, eggs and water. Make a well in center of flour mixture and stir in liquid, mixing well. Put a clean towel over the bowl and let stand for 3 1/2 hours. Knead dough for about 3 minutes. Turn out onto a floured surface and roll out to 4 inch thickness. Cut pieces in triangular shapes and fry in hot fat until golden brown.

## ALL BRAN BREAD

| | |
|---|---|
| *1 egg, beaten* | *1 1/2 cups all bran* |
| *1/2 tsp. salt* | *1 1/2 cups all purpose flour* |
| *1/2 cup white sugar* | *1 1/2 cups sour milk* |
| *1/2 cup molasses* | *1 tsp. baking soda* |

Combine all dry ingredients and make a well in center. Add egg, molasses and milk. Mix well and pour in a greased loaf pan.
Bake at 325 F for 35 to 40 minutes.

## WILD RICE
## GAMEBIRD STUFFING

| | |
|---|---|
| *2 cups wild rice (cooked)* | *2 tbsp. crisp bacon* |
| *2/3 cups stewed tomatoes* | *1/2 tsp. salt* |
| *1 tsp. minced onion* | *1/2 tsp. pepper* |

Mix all ingredients together. Stuffing is good with fowl.

## PARTRIDGE STUFFING

4 cups dried bread, cut in 1/2 inch cubes
3/4 cup celery, finely chopped
1/4 cup green pepper, chopped
1 small onion, finely chopped

1 tbsp. minced parsley
1/2 tsp. salt
1/4 cup butter
2 eggs

Combine bread, celery , pepper, onion, and seasonings.  Melt butter; remove from heat.  Stir in unbeaten eggs and add to bread mixture.  Toss lightly.

## CRANBERRY AND RAISIN STUFFING

1/4 cup butter
5 cups fine stale bread crumbs
1 cup chopped fresh cranberries
1/4 cup sugar

1/4 cup raisins
1 tsp. salt
1 tsp. grated rind

In a bowl mix cranberries and sugar.  Allow to set a few minutes. In a separate bowl mix melted butter and crumbs together.  Then add combines sugared cranberries and all remaining ingredients, using just enough water to bind mixture.  Makes enough for 5 to 6 pounds.
Recipe can be doubled.

# CORN BREAD STUFFING

| | |
|---|---|
| 4 tbsp. butter | 3 cups corn bread, crumbled |
| 1 onion, diced | 1 cup pecans, chopped |
| 2 stalks celery, diced | 1/2 tsp. thyme |

Melt butter in skillet.  Saute onion and celery until soft. Combine corn bread and pecans in a bowl and toss with the sauteed vegetables and butter from the skillet.

Sprinkle with thyme and toss again.

✳

# CHEESE STUFFING FOR FISH

| | |
|---|---|
| One medium onion, chopped | 2 tbsp. parsley |
| 1/4 cup margarine or bacon drippings | 2 tbsp. mustard |
| 2 cups bread crumbs | 1/2 tsp. pepper |
| 1/2 cup cheese grated | |

Cook onion in margarine until tender.   In a bowl combine bread crumbs, cheese, parsley, mustard, salt and pepper.

Add onions and bacon drippings and toss slightly.

✳

# 200.

## HOMEMADE FISH BATTER

1 1/2 cups all-purpose flour
3 tsp. baking powder

1 cup milk
2 eggs, well beaten

1 tsp. salt

Mix and sift dry ingredients.  Add milk to eggs.  Pour liquid into dry mixture, and beat until smooth. Dip fish pieces into mixture and deep fry in oil or fat until golden brown.

## EASY FISH BATTER

1 pkg. crushed crackers
2 eggs, beaten
1/2 cup milk

Mix together in a bowl eggs and milk.  On an appropriate size plate spread out cracker crumbs. Dip fish pieces in egg and milk mixture. Roll fish in the crushed cracker crumbs and fry.

# · CHAPTER EIGHT ·

# EDIBLE WILD PLANTS , NUTS , BERRIES AND WILD BAKING

There are hundreds of wild plants that are good eating. Indians relied on these various plants for many of their basic food staples.

The illustrations provided here are a general aid to identification only. Do not attempt to eat something new to you based on these illustrations alone. Many different plants appear the same to the untrained eye. Please consult with an experienced friend or other resource person before eating a plant for the first time. **Never eat anything you are unsure about.**

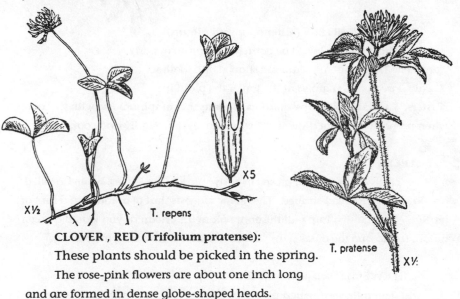

**CLOVER , RED (Trifolium pratense):**
These plants should be picked in the spring.

The rose-pink flowers are about one inch long and are formed in dense globe-shaped heads.

**WHITE (Trifolium repens):** These flowers are white with pink bases and the leaflets are heart-shaped and formed in groups of three.

The roots, stems and flowers of the clover are all edible, but as with all wild flowers, should be cleaned and soaked in salted water for a couple of hours. Use in the recipes that follow.

LAMB'S
QUARTERS

A. syriaca

X 4

X ½

MILKWEED

X ½

X 4

## LAMB'S QUARTERS ( Chenopodium album)

These plants should be gathered in spring or early
summer.  The leaves are diamond shaped and toothed.
A pale   green flower grows at the top of the plant in
clusters. The flavor of lambs' quarters suggests that of spinach. As with spinach,
when preparing, do not drown; just wash leaves thoroughly and cook.

## LEEKS

Leeks are best when picked in early spring.  The leaves, when unrolled,
are flat and lancehead-shaped.  The flavor suggests that of onion with a hint of
garlic.  When cultivating, pull the entire plant and clean as you would a green
onion, (removing the outer skin).  Eat raw or use for flavoring in cooking.

## MILKWEED (Asclepias syriaca)

The milkweed, when picked in early spring, is a whitish-green color.
They may grow to a height of 5 feet.  The seedbeds grow from 3 to 5 inches long
and are covered with soft spines and hair.  The stalks emit a milky substance when
broken.

Pick stalks and seedbeds wash thoroughly.  Boil for 1 minute; strain, and
repeat at least 3 times.  Boil once again for 10 minutes.  Drain, season and serve.

## COMMON MORELS

Common morels appear in May. In appearance they resemble long, tiny sponges and have hollow white stems. The cap has irregular pits like that of a honeycomb. To prepare, soak in cold salted water for 2 to 3 hours, before using in any recipe.

## STINGING NETTLES (Laportea Canadensis)

Gather these plants in spring or early summer, wearing gloves, as this plant releases an irritating oil, rich in formatic acid when touched. The stinging properties are eliminated through cooking and drying. Collect the young top leaves and steam until tender. Serve with butter. Do not overcook. They need only cook for about 1 minute. The leaves can also be dried and used for tea. The stinging nettle suggests the flavor of spinach.

## PUFFBALLS

All puffballs with white flesh are good eating. Avoid picking the ones that are over-ripe. These will fall apart when touched or if cut open, the center will appear yellow to greenish-brown. In preparing, if the puffball is small; simply scrape off the soil, rinse, and wipe with a damp cloth. Large puffballs should be peeled. The flavor suggests that of a mushroom.

## COMMON PURSLANE (Porulaca oleracea)

This plant may be gathered all through the summer months. In appearance the stems are a reddish color, the leaves are small and paddle-shaped, and the flowers are small, 5 petaled and yellow.

When the leaves are used, first wash well and then they can be used raw in salads are cooked. This is an excellent substitute for cucumbers.

The seeds can be ground into meal and mixed with flour to bake breads or boiled and eaten as porridge.

## WILD ROSE ( Rosa family)

This thorny plant grows in thickets of 4 to 6 feet tall and has oval-shaped, toothed leaves 2 to 4 inches long. The wild rose is a light red 5 petaled flower. The fruit can be eaten raw and suggests a flavor of apples.

AS A SWEETENER: The seeds must be pulverized, boiled and strained through cheesecloth, to use as a syrup. AS A TEA: Steep flowers for 5 minutes in boiling water and sweeten with wild honey.

### WATER CRESS (Nasturtium officinale)

This plant should be gathered in the spring and summer. In appearance the leaves a shiny, dark green with rounded lobes, and the flowers are white, and grow in clusters.

Water Cress is popular because of its superior taste to any kind of lettuce.

To cultivate, snip or pinch off at the waters' surface. Do not pull up the entire plant. Wash thoroughly and use in salads or as a fresh or cooked vegetable.

### WOOD SORREL ( Oxalis europea)

This plant should be picked in the summer. The flower closely resembles the clover, as the flowers are compounded in 3's and close at night. Flowers run in color from yellow to purple and always have 5 petals. The stems are long and juicy. The wood sorrel has a delicate lemony flavor.

Wash thoroughly and add to soups, stews, or mix in salads.

The stems are full of moisture and make a good thirst quencher by simply nibbling.

### YELLOW PONDLILY ( Nuphar variegatum)

This plant is gathered in the summer and fall, using a canoe or boat. The leaves are large and oval-shaped, with a deep curve at the heart-shaped base. The large & showy flowers are flattened globes made up of half a dozen thick golden sepals arching over the petals. The petals and sepals will rot away, leaving a large fleshy green capsule filled with numerous seeds. Eventually, the pulpy flesh of the fruit disintegrates to release the edible seeds. The taste of the seeds resemble that of the chestnut and the roots, the taste of a potato.

PREPARATION: Remove outer shell that encloses the seeds; boil seeds to make a gruel, or parch in a hot frying pan until seeds swell and pop open slightly. These cracked seeds can be eaten as is or pounded into meal and used to make bread and porridge. The meal can also be used as a soup thickener. The seeds can be dried and stored in a cool, dark place. The potato-like roots are also delicious edibles. Their overpowering taste can be lessened by boiling in two changes of water and seasoned.

# 205.

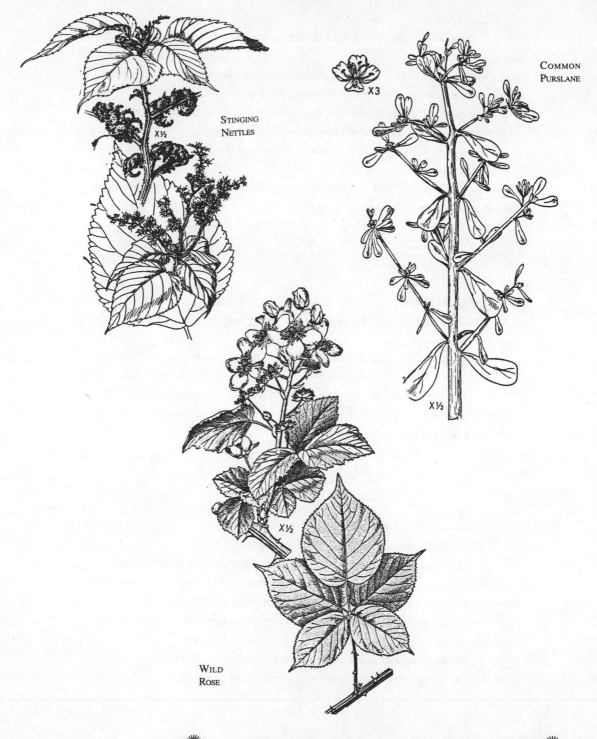

STINGING
NETTLES

X½

X3

COMMON
PURSLANE

X½

WILD
ROSE

X½

**CATTAILS:**

Cattails can grow to a height of 10 feet. They are found in many marshy areas.

CATTAIL SHOOTS: Are easily pulled and have a syrupy core which is eaten like celery, cooked or raw. The spikes taste similar to corn.

YELLOW POLLEN: When dried and sifted can be used as flour; either along or mixed half & half with conventional flour.

ROOTS & ROOTSHOOTS: Sprouts: Boiled are good with butter or when cooked with meat.

CATTAIL POTATOES: Are found below the shoots and when peeled can be used raw in salads or cooked as potatoes.

**DANDELIONS**

WINE: Flowers should be washed thoroughly and wine preparation began immediately.

ROOTS: Can be used like chicory for a non-caffinated coffee substitute.

The cooked leaves suggest a flavor of spinach. They should be picked before the flowers appear; otherwise they have to be boiled twice to remove the bitterness from them.

**FIDDLEHEADS**

Fiddleheads gain their name because of their shape. The best time to cultivate this plant is before it reaches a height of approximately 6 inches, and appear still curled and rusty in color. When picking, pick close to the root.

To prepare, remove rusty colored skim and wash in warm water. Let stand in cold water for 30 minutes.

Serving suggestions: Steam or saute fiddleheads and serve with butter and bacon. The plant suggests a flavor of broccoli or asparagus.

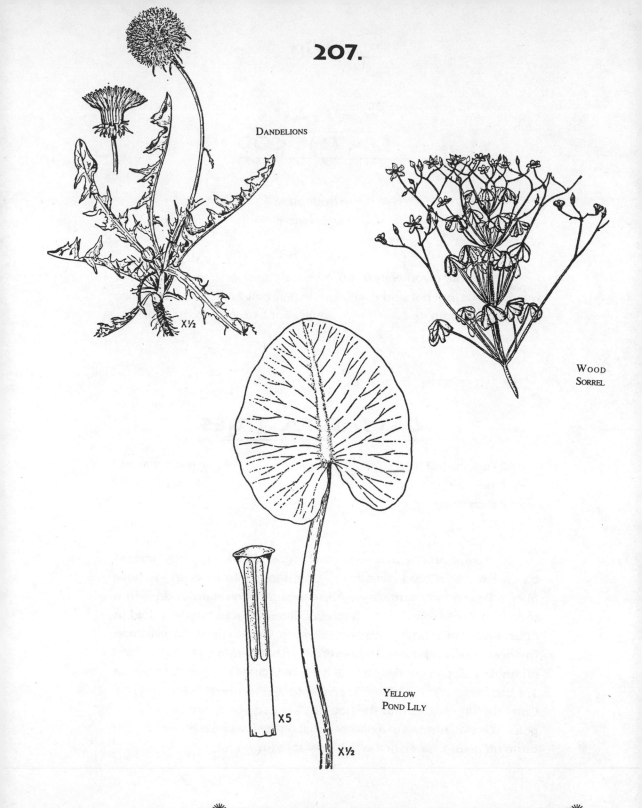

**207.**

Dandelions

Wood
Sorrel

Yellow
Pond Lily

X½

X5

X½

# CATTAILS
# ON THE COB

*cattail spikes*
*water butter*

Gather green cattail spikes of early spring. Clean off in cold water. Place in a pot and cover with water, boil for 10 to 15 minutes. When done, drain and serve with butter. Eat like corn on the cob.

✳

# CATTAIL PASTRIES

*2 cups cattail flour*          *vegetable oil*
*1 tsp. salt*                   *honey*
*2 cups water*

Scrape and clean several cattail roots. Place on lightly greased cookie sheet in a 200 F oven to dry overnight. Skin roots and remove fibers. Pound roots until fine. Allow to stand overnight to dry. In a saucepan, bring salted water to a boil. Remove from heat and fold in flour. Beat until mixture forms a thick paste. Cool to room temperature. In a deep fryer, heat about 3 inches of oil to a temperature of 400 F or until oil smokes. Spoon out dough onto a floured cookie sheet to form a cake 1/4 inch thick. Cut ribbons 1/2 inch wide and about 5 inches long. Carefully lift ribbons into the hot oil. Deep-fry for 5 minutes or until golden brown, turning at least once. Lift out and set on a paper towel to drain off grease. Serve hot with honey spread on top.

## SESHELT CHOWDER

4 big cattail roots, roasted
and diced

5 cups water

1 1/2 lbs. roughly cut salmon, fresh

1/4 tsp. fresh pepper

2 tsp. salt

Simmer the cattail roots for 40 minutes. Add remaining ingredients and simmer another 10 minutes.

❋

# DANDELION
# GREENS SUPREME

1 tbsp. margarine

4 cups dandelion greens, chopped

2 tbsp. beef broth

1/4 cup onions, chopped

1/4 cup bacon, fried

2 tbsp. heavy cream

Melt margarine in a deep skillet. Stir in dandelion greens, onions and beef broth. Cover and cook over medium heat for 10 to 12 minutes, stirring occasionally. Mix in heavy cream and bacon. Cook until most of the liquid disappears. Season with salt and pepper.

## DANDELION GREENS

4 cups dandelion greens, washed          2 tbsp. margarine
1/2 cup onion, diced                     salt and pepper to taste

Immerse dandelion greens in salted boiling water. Cook until water returns to a rapid boil. Drain and chop. Saute onions in margarine and mix in greens. Season with salt and pepper.

## CREAM OF FIDDLEHEAD
## SOUP WITH MUSHROOMS

1 lb. fiddleheads                        1 can beef consomme
1 can cream of mushroom soup                      1 tsp. salt
2 cups milk                                  1/2 tsp. pepper

Clean rust and woolly coating from the fiddleheads by rubbing them between the hands and wash under running water. Drop fiddleheads into 1 quart of boiling salted water and boil for 10 minutes. Remove from heat and immerse in cold water for 2 minutes. Drain and set aside. In clean saucepan, bring mushroom soup and milk to a boil, over medium heat. Reduce heat to low. Add fiddleheads and cook for 20 minutes. Place a fine sieve over a large bowl and pour hot soup through. With a wooden spoon, rub fiddleheads and mushrooms through as well. Pour mixture from the bowl back into saucepan. Add consomme and simmer over low heat for 5 minutes. Season to taste. If too thick, add a little milk. Garnish with small pieces of fiddleheads and chopped parsley.

# MARINATED FIDDLEHEADS

2 quarts fiddleheads

3 cups water

juice of 1 lemon

5 tbsp. vinegar

1/2 cup oil

1 tsp. salt

2 stalks celery, chopped

1 stalk fennel

In a saucepan combine water, lemon juice, vinegar oil, salt, fennel and celery. Bring to a boil. Add fiddleheads and simmer 20 minutes, or until fiddleheads are tender. Drain, cool and place in refrigerator until ready to be served.

# CLOVER SOUP

2 cups clover flowers and leaves

1 onion, chopped

3 tbsp. butter

2 pints water

3 potatoes, peeled and quartered

salt and pepper to taste

parsley

cheddar cheese, grated

Clean and dip clover flowers and leaves in cold salted water. Remove and cut into pieces. In a large saucepan, saute flowers, leaves and onions in butter. When all is softened add water then potatoes and season with salt and pepper. Cook gently for 20 minutes. Drain the cooking liquid and save it. Puree potato mixture and dilute with the cooking liquid, stirring constantly. Bring to a boil, then reduce heat and simmer for 3 minutes. Garnish with parsley and sprinkle with grated cheese.

# HOMEMADE
# HONEY

| | |
|---|---|
| 80 white clover blossoms | 10 cups sugar |
| 40 red clover blossoms | 3 cups water |

*petals from 5 roses (not too highly scented)*
*1/2 teaspoon powdered alum*

Boil sugar, water and alum together for 5 minutes. Then pour over blossoms and petals, allowing it to stand for 20 minutes. Strain through cheese cloth into sterilized containers and seal tightly. It can be kept for years.

# LAMB S QUARTERS
# FRITTERS

| | |
|---|---|
| 1 quart of lamb's quarters, washed | 2 eggs, separated |
| 1/2 tsp. nutmeg | |
| 1 tbsp. butter | oil for deep frying |

*1/2 cup parmesan cheese, grated*

Boil lamb's quarters for 10 minutes. Strain and then chop. Place in a bowl and sprinkle nutmeg over the leaves. Stir in 2 egg yolks and lastly the parmesan cheese. Allow mixture to cool.

Beat egg whites and stir into mixture. Drop by spoonfuls into hot oil. Fry until golden brown on both sides. Serve immediately.

# LAMB'S QUARTERS
# AND BACON

*5 or 6 strips bacon*
*2 cups lamb's quarters leaves,*
*washed and chopped*

Fry bacon until crisp. Remove from frying pan leaving 2 tablespoons of fat. Add lamb's quarters leaves and fry for about 5 minutes or until leaves are tender. Crumble bacon pieces and mix in with the lamb's quarters leaves. Serve.

TYPHA

CATTAILS

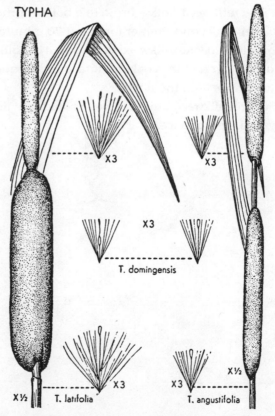

T. domingensis

T. latifolia    T. angustifolia

# GLAZED
# MILKWEED STALKS

*1 dozen young milkweed stalks*　　　　*1/2 tsp. salt*
*1 1/2 cups chicken stock*　　　　　　*1/4 tsp. pepper*
*4 tbsp. butter*　　　　　　　　　　*2 tbsp. parsley*
*2 tbsp. sugar*

Clean and peel young milkweed stalks and cut into 2 inch lengths.  In a 12 inch skillet, combine chicken stock, butter, sugar, salt, pepper and milkweed stalks.  Bring to a boil over moderate heat.

Cover skillet and simmer for about 20 minutes, shaking the pan occasionally to roll the milkweed stalks about in liquid. When milkweed stalks are tender and the cooking fluid is brown and shiny, the dish is ready to remove from the stove.

Be sure milkweed stalks are well-coated with liquid.  Sprinkle with parsley and serve at once.

## ALL FOR YOU MORELS

*1 lb. morels*
*1 onion, sliced thin*
*2 tbsp. flour*

*1 cup sour cream*
*1/4 cup milk*
*salt and pepper*

*3 tbsp. butter*

In a frying pan, saute onion in 2 tablespoons of butter. In another pan, melt one tablespoon of butter and stir in flour. Add milk and stir until smooth. Pour onions into the mixture and add morels. Season with salt and pepper. Then add 1/2 of the sour cream, stirring thoroughly, but gently. Cook over medium heat for about 10 minutes, then add remaining sour cream. Heat another 5 minutes and serve.

## CORNY MORELS

*morels, as many as gathered*
*butter*
*1 tin of corn nibbles*
*1 small green pepper, sliced thin*
*1 tbsp. soya sauce (optional)*

Fry morels and green pepper in melted butter allowing morels to remain plump. Stir in soya sauce. In a saucepan, heat corn nibbles and then mix in mushrooms and green pepper. Serve.

# CREAMED NETTLES

2 cups water
1/2 tsp. salt
2 cups nettle leaves, washed
3 tbsp. butter or margarine
1 tbsp. flour

1 tsp. sugar
1/2 cup cream
salt and pepper to taste
1/4 tsp. nutmeg
1/4 cup almonds, crushed

Boil nettle leaves for 2 or 3 minutes. Then, drain and chop. Cook nettles in a saucepan with melted butter for 3 minutes. Stir in flour. Add cream and cook for an additional 5 minutes, until thickened. Stir in sugar and seasonings and sprinkle almonds on top. Serve.

# NETTLE SOUP

2 cups nettle leaves
2 tbsp. butter
1 tsp. onion, minced

4 cups chicken broth
salt
sour cream

To pick nettles, wear a pair of gloves and use a pair of shears. Pick enough so that you will have 2 cups of tender top leaves, firmly packed. Pour boiling water over nettles to remove prickles. Drain and chop. Melt butter in saucepan and saute onion for 1 minute. Add broth, nettles, and salt to taste. Simmer a few minutes. Serve topped with a spoonful of sour cream.

# PUFFBALLS

# WITH BACON

| | |
|---|---|
| 1 lb. bacon | butter or margarine |
| 1 large puffball, sliced thin | salt and pepper to taste |

Cook bacon, drain, set aside, and keep warm.  In a skillet, melt a generous amount of butter or margarine over medium heat. Place slices of puffball in skillet and sprinkle with salt and pepper.  When slices have browned on one side, turn and brown other side.  Serve with bacon.

# CREAM PUFFBALLS

| | |
|---|---|
| 3 cups of puffball, diced | 1/4 tsp. nutmeg |
| 1 tbsp. butter | flour |
| 1/2 cup heavy cream | paprika |
| salt and pepper to taste | |

Saute puffball cubes over low heat.  Sprinkle lightly with flour. Then, add cream, salt, pepper and nutmeg. Cover and continue cooking over low heat for 10 to 15 minutes.  Garnish with paprika and serve on toast.

# PURSLANE
# AND FRIED EGGS

1/2 cup water

2 cups purslane leaves

1/4 cup butter

1 tsp. white wine vinegar

salt and pepper to taste

4 eggs

2 tbsp. butter

Bring water to a boil and add purslane leaves. Reduce heat and simmer for about 5 minutes. Drain. In a skillet melt 1/4 cup butter and add purslane leaves, vinegar, salt and pepper. Fry for about 5 minutes over medium heat. In an other skillet, melt 2 tablespoons of butter and fry eggs as desired. When cooked, pour purslane leaves over top and serve.

# PURSLANE GREENS

1/4 cup water

2 cups purslane leaves

2 tbsp. butter or margarine

1/4 cup dry white wine

3 tbsp. lemon juice

1 tbsp. worcestershire sauce

salt and pepper to taste

Bring water to a boil and add purslane leaves. Reduce heat and simmer for 5 minutes. Drain and chop. In a heavy frying pan, melt butter and add all the ingredients. Stir gently and heat thoroughly. Serve hot.

## ROSE FRITTERS

rose petals, fresh
brandy
1 egg

3/4 cup flour

1/2 tsp. salt
1/2 cup milk
powdered sugar

Dip rose petals in brandy, then in a batter made with egg, flour, salt and milk.  Fry in deep fat at 375 F for 1 minute.  Drain and dust with powdered sugar.

## ROSE HIP JELLY

4 quarts ripe rose hips
2 quarts water

1/2 cup lemon juice

1 pkg. pectin crystals
5 cups sugar

Simmer rose hips in water until soft.  Crush to mash, and strain through a jelly bag.  Should make about 4 cups of rose hip juice.

Add to juice, lemon juice and pectin crystals and stir until mixture comes to a hard boil.  Stir sugar in at once.  Bring to a full rolling boil and boil for 1 minute, stirring constantly.

Remove jelly from heat and skim off foam with metal spoon. Pour into hot sterilized jars.

## STEWED WATER CRESS

| | |
|---|---|
| *1 lb. water cress* | *4 tbsp. flour* |
| *1/2 cup heavy cream* | *1/2 tsp. white pepper* |
| *1 1/2 cups milk* | *1/2 tsp. salt* |
| *4 tbsp. butter* | |

In a saucepan, melt butter over a moderate heat. Remove from heat and stir in flour. Pour milk and cream in stirring constantly. Cook over low heat until the sauce is smooth and thick. Season with salt and pepper. Parboil water cress for about 5 minutes and drain. Then chop very fine. Add to sauce and heat through. Serve with parsley flakes as a garnish.

## WOOD SORREL SAUCE

| | |
|---|---|
| *2 tbsp. butter* | *1 tbsp. white vinegar* |
| *1/4 cup green onions, chopped* | *1/2 cup heavy cream* |
| *1/2 cup flour* | *1 tbsp. sugar* |
| *1 cup beef stock* | *1/2 cup wood sorrel leaves and tubers, chopped* |

In a saucepan, melt butter. When a nutty odor is emitted, add onion and cook until lightly browned. Add flour, stirring constantly until mixture is lightly browned. Add beef stock, sugar and vinegar. Bring to a boil, reduce heat and simmer for 20 minutes or until sauce is smooth. Pour through a sieve. Return sauce to saucepan and add wood sorrel leaves and tubers. Stir in cream and simmer until hot. Serve with beef.

## SORREL SOUP

1/2 cup sorrel leaves         2 egg yolks, well beaten

4 cups chicken broth         2 tbsp. sherry

Heat chicken broth and add sorrel. Simmer for 5 minutes. Slowly pour liquid over the beaten egg yolks, whipping briskly to prevent curdling. Return to sauce pan and heat but do not boil. Add sherry and serve.

## GOLDEN POND

## LILY STEW

2 lbs. stewing beef         salt and pepper to taste

12 lily roots, cleaned and sliced         2 cups water

3 tbsp. butter         1/3 cup dry red wine

6 green onions, chopped    2 tbsp. flour, mixed with 1/4 cup water

In a saucepan, brown onions and stewing beef in melted butter. Add lily roots, water, salt and pepper. Cover and bring to a boil, then reduce heat and simmer for 3 to 4 hours. In the last 15 minutes of cooking time, add wine and stir in flour and water mixture to thicken stew.

# WATER LILY

# POPCORN

*1/2 lb. water lily seeds*
*2 tbsp. butter*
*1 1/2 tsp. salt*

To separate seeds from floaters, break away green holsters of pods and dump all the seeds into water of a 4 quart pot. Allow to set for 6 to 8 hours after which time seeds will separate from floaters and will sink to the bottom of the pot. Skim off surface and drain water through a sieve. Place seeds on a cookie sheet and allow seeds to dry. If dried in an oven, set at 150 F otherwise if hotter, seeds will pop. Melt butter in a saucepan, add salt and seeds and cook over high heat as your ordinary popcorn.

✳

# SUMAC JELLY

*2 quarts crimson sumac heads*
*water*
*3 cups apple juice*
*1 pkg. pectin crystals*
*9 cups sugar*

Wash sumac and cover with water, and simmer for about 15 minutes. Should make 5 cups of clear crimson sumac juice.

Add juice, apple juice and pectin crystals and stir until mixture comes to a boil. Then stir in sugar and boil hard for a minute, stirring constantly. Remove from heat and skim off foam. Pour at once into sterilized jars.

# 223.
# RASPBERRY OR
# BLACKBERRY
# DUMPLINGS

3 pints blackberries or raspberries     3 tbsp. sugar
3/4 cup water     1 tsp. salt
1 cup sugar     1 egg
1 1/2 tbsp. margarine     3 1/2 tbsp. baking powder
2 cups flour     milk

Combine first four ingredients in a saucepan and set aside. Set together flour, sugar, salt and baking powder. Add egg and mix well. Stir in enough milk to make a stiff batter.

Place saucepan on the heat and bring mixture to a boil. Drop flour mixture in by tablespoonsful. Cover and cook for 15 to 20 minutes. Can be served with ice cream or thick cream.

# SUMACADE

6 to 8 medium sized sumac fruit clusters
6 cups water
1/2 cup sugar

Wash sumac fruit and break off the main stems of clusters. Place in a large saucepan with water and bruise fruit thoroughly until water turns pink. Remove larger pieces and strain as you would to make jelly. Add sugar and stir until dissolved. Serve cold as is or mix it half and half with other fruit juices.

## WILD APPLE SAUCE

*4 lbs. wild crab apples (core them
but do not peel) cut into slices
8 oz. maple sugar (1/2 pound)
4 cups water*

Place all ingredients together in a large saucepan. Bring to a boil
and reduce heat. Simmer 50 minutes, stirring frequently.

## TRADITIONAL

## CRANBERRY SAUCE

*1 1/2 lbs. wild high bush cranberries
or domestic cranberry
2 cups maple sugar
1 1/2 cups birch sap or spring
water*

Place all ingredients in a large saucepan and bring to a boil.
Reduce heat and simmer 25 to 30 minutes.
Cool and serve with wild meat.

# WILD CRANBERRY
# CONSERVE

| | |
|---|---|
| 1 quart cranberries | 1 lb. raisins |
| 1 1/2 cups water | 1 large orange, sliced |
| | 1 1/2 lbs. sugar |

Wash and pick over cranberries, then cook them in water until they have burst. Add all remaining ingredients and cook for 25 minutes. Stir often. Place in small sterilized jars and seal.

# WILD CRANBERRY JUICE

| | |
|---|---|
| 2 cups cranberries | 1/2 cup apple juice |
| 3 cups water | 2 tbsp. lemon juice |
| | 1/2 cup sugar |

Cook cranberries in water for 5 minutes. Strain through cheese-cloth. Boil juice and add sugar, stirring until sugar is dissolved, about 2 minutes. Add lemon juice and chill.

# WILD CRANBERRY

## SAUCE

*4 cups cranberries*
*2 cups water*
*2 cups sugar*

Wash and pick over cranberries, cook them in water until berries burst. Strain, rubbing as much as possible of the pulp through a sieve. Add sugar and stir until dissolved.

Boil rapidly for 12 to 15 minutes. Chill.

✳

# ELDERBERRY CATSUP

*2 quarts elderberries*          *1 tbsp. allspice*
*vinegar to cover*               *1 tbsp. cloves*
*1 cup sugar*                    *1/4 tsp. cayenne pepper*
          *1 tsp. cinnamon*

Cook elderberries in vinegar until berries burst. Put berries through a food press or sieve, add sugar, cinnamon, allspice, cloves and pepper. Simmer until thickens. Pour into sterilized jars and seal.

# ELDERFLOWER
# FRITTERS

| | |
|---|---|
| elderflowers, washed and drained | 1/4 tsp. pepper |
| 1/2 cup flour | 1 tsp. melted butter |
| 2 eggs, well beaten | 1 tbsp. brandy |
| 3/4 tsp. salt | powdered sugar |

Combine eggs, flour, salt, pepper, butter and brandy together. Beat well.  Dip flowers in batter and fry in deep fat at 350 F until crisp and brown.  Drain on paper towels. Sprinkle with powdered sugar and serve hot.

# WILD BLUEBERRY
# COOKIES

| | |
|---|---|
| 2 cups flour | 1 cup sugar |
| 2 tsp. baking powder | 1 1/2 tsp. lemon rind, grated |
| 1/2 tsp. salt | 1 egg |
| 3/4 cup wild blueberries | 1/4 cup milk |
| 1/2 cup shortening | |

## DIRECTIONS

Combine flour, baking powder and salt; stir in blueberries. Cream shortening until soft, gradually beat in sugar, then lemon rind and egg. Add flour mixture alternately with milk, beating until smooth after each addition. Drop from teaspoon onto greased cookie sheet. Bake at 375 F for 8 to 12 minutes.

# CURRIED FRUIT WITH

# WILD BLUEBERRIES

*1 cup wild blueberries*          *1/3 cup butter, melted*
*1 cup raspberries*                *3 tsp. curry powder*
*1 cup pears*                      *3/4 cup brown sugar*

*1 cup peaches*

Place fruit into a shallow baking dish. Combine butter, curry powder and brown sugar together. Pour over fruit. Marinate overnight. Bake at 350 F for 1 hour.

# WILD BLUEBERRY
## PANCAKES

| | |
|---|---|
| 1 1/2 cups all-purpose flour | 3 eggs |
| 1 1/2 cups whole wheat flour | 1/2 cup margarine, melted |
| 2 tsp. baking powder | 1 cup plain yogurt |
| 2 tsp. baking soda | 1 cup milk |
| 1/2 cup granulated sugar | 2 cups wild blueberries |
| 1 1/2 tsp. salt | |

Combine all dry ingredients in a large bowl. In a separate bowl, beat together eggs, margarine, yogurt and milk.

Make a well in center of dry ingredients and stir in egg mixture until blended but still lumpy.

Spoon 1/4 cup of batter onto an oiled, hot skillet and sprinkle with a few blueberries. When bubbles form and hold in batter, flip and cook until bottom is browned.

Serve with butter and maple syrup.

# HUCKLEBERRY

# MUFFINS

| | |
|---|---|
| *1 cup huckleberries* | *2 eggs* |
| *1/2 cup brown sugar* | *4 tbsp. margarine, melted* |
| *2 cups all-purpose flour* | *1 tsp. vanilla* |
| *1 tbsp. baking powder* | *1/4 cup milk* |
| *1/2 tsp. salt* | *1/4 cup syrup* |

Combine sugar and huckleberries. Stir in flour, baking powder and salt. In a separate bowl, beat together eggs, milk, vanilla, margarine and syrup.

Combine the two mixtures, using a fork to stir. Do not over mix. Fill well greased muffin tins, three quarters full.

Bake at 450 F for 20 to 25 minutes.

✳

# HUCKLEBERRY CRISP

| | |
|---|---|
| 1/3 cup sugar | 1/4 tsp. nutmeg |
| 2 tbsp. cornstarch | 1 tbsp. lemon juice |
| 1/4 tsp. cinnamon | 4 cups huckleberries, sweetened |
| 1/4 tsp. salt | 1 cup huckleberry juice (drained from fruit) |

Combine sugar, cornstarch, salt and spices in a saucepan. Add lemon and huckleberry juices and stir until smooth.

Cook over low heat until thickened and clear, stirring constantly. Stir in huckleberries and pour into a greased baking dish.

## TOPPING:

1/3 cup butter or margarine
1 cup brown sugar, firmly packed
2 tbsp. flour
3 cups corn flakes

Melt butter in a saucepan. Combine sugar and flour and add to butter. Cook, stirring constantly over low heat for 3 minutes. Add cornflakes mixing quickly until they are coated with syrup. Sprinkle over the huckleberry mixture and bake at 400 F for 30 minutes or until topping is crisp and golden brown. Serve warm or cold.

# WILD RASPBERRY
# BREAD PUDDING

*10 cups wild raspberries cleaned, dried*
*2 cups sugar*
*12 slices homemade white bread*
*2 cups heavy cream*

In a large bowl, sprinkle sugar over raspberries. Toss berries very lightly until all sugar has dissolved. Cover and set aside. Cut slice of bread to fit the bottom of a deep 2 quart bowl.

Trim 8 or 9 slices of bread into wedges about 4 inches at the top and 3 inches across bottom. Line sides of bowl with wedges, overlapping each one by about 1/2 inch.

Pour fruit into the bowl and cover top completely with the rest of bread. Cover top of bowl with a flat plate and place a weight on top of plate. Place in refrigerator for at least 12 hours.

Remove mold by quickly inverting it onto a chilled serving plate. The mold should slide out easily. Whip cream in a large chilled bowl until it holds its shape. With a spatula, cover mold on the outside and top. Serve chilled.

# ADOBE BREAD

*(makes 2 loaves)*

| | |
|---|---|
| 1 (1/4 oz.) package dry yeast | 1 teaspoon salt |
| 1/4 cup warm water | 4 1/2 cups flour |
| 2 tablespoons melted lard or shortening | 1 cup water |

Soften the yeast in the warm water in a large mixing bowl. Then mix the melted lard or shortening and the salt

Add the flour alternately with the water, sifting the flour in a little at a time and beating well after each addition to make a smooth mixture. You will probably have to knead in the final cup of flour.

Shape the dough into a ball, place in a greased bowl, brush lightly with melted lard or shortening, cover with a dry cloth, and set in a warm place to rise for about 1 hour.

When the dough has doubled in bulk, punch it down, turn onto a floured board and knead for about 5 minutes. Divide into two equal parts and shape into two round loaves on a well oiled board or greased baking tin.

Cover the loaves with a dry cloth, set in a warm place, and let rise for 15 minutes.

Bake the bread in a hot oven, 400 F., for 50 minutes or until loaves are lightly browned and sound hollow when thumped. Cool ; cut into wedges before serving.

# WASNA (CORN CAKE)

*5 cups parched corn (use white flour corn)*
*3 cups sugar*
*2 cups tallow or shortening*

Grind the corn well. Place in a large mixing bowl. Add the other ingredients, mix well and place the wasna in an oblong pan to serve.

✳

# CACTUS SALAD

*1 (7 1/4 oz.) can natural cactus in salt water drained*
*1 (7 oz.) can pimento, drained*

## DRESSING:

*3 tbsp. salad oil*              *2 tbsp. tarragon vinegar*
*1 scallion, washed and minced*
*1 clove garlic, peeled and crushed*
*1/8 tsp. fresh ground pepper*

Arrange a bed of cactus on a small platter. Slice the pimento into julienne strips and place over the cactus. Mix together the dressing ingredients and pour over salad. Marinate in the refrigerator an hour before serving.

# SQUASH SOUP

*1 - crooked neck squash or 1/2 Mother Hubbard squash*
*10 medium potatoes (quartered)*
*1/2 lbs. salt pork (sliced)*
*1 can (#10) whole kernel corn or 3 cups dried corn.*

Boil the salt pork for 1/2 hour then add the other ingredients.

✳

# TIMSILA SOUP
# (WILD TURNIP)

*2 lbs. dry wild turnips*
*pinch of pepper*
*2 lbs. potatoes*
*1/4 cup flour*
*1 tsp. salt*

# MOTHER'S
# VEGETABLE SOUP

6 fresh icicle radishes          1 small onion
1 lb. dried meat or stew meat    3 carrots
4 large potatoes                 salt and pepper seasoning

Dice the carrots. Add the carrots and meat to 3 quarts of water. Boil 1/2 hour. Quarter the potatoes. Dice the onions and radishes. Add to the stew. Boil until soft.

# SMOKED
# SALMON SOUP

1 lb. smoked salmon          6 cups water
2 tsp. salt                  1/8 tsp. pepper
4 potatoes, diced            3/4 cup young spinach

Break salmon into bite-sized pieces, add diced potatoes, water, pepper and salt. Bring to boil, reduce heat and cook until potatoes are done (about 20 minutes). Add spinach, simmer 5 minutes longer.

# SOUTHERN CHOWDER

1 tbsp. oil
1 large onion, chopped
1 medium potato, sliced
3 beets, sliced
5 cups water
1 tsp. salt

1 cracked shin bone
1 cup shredded cabbage
2 summer squash, sliced
3 carrots, sliced
2 green chiles, chopped
1/4 tsp. pepper

Bring water, salt, pepper and soup bone to boil, simmer 45 minutes.  Saute onion in oil.  Add onion and remaining ingredients.  Simmer until done, remove bone and serve.

❋

# BLACK BEAN SOUP

1 cup leeks, sliced
2 cloves garlic minced
1/2 cup water

1/3 cup oil
2 lbs. cooked black beans
salt and pepper to taste

Saute leeks and garlic in oil until soft.  Mash half of beans in a saucepan.  Add remaining ingredients.  Simmer 40 minutes, stirring occasionally.

## OYSTER SOUP

2 quarts oysters                    2 quarts water
2 onions, chopped                   1/2 tsp. salt
1/4 tsp. pepper                     2 tbsp. butter
2 tbsp. flour                       1 cup cream

Wash oysters and boil in salted water until opened. Remove oysters and shell. Strain liquid, add onion and pepper, cooking until onion is done. Form flour and butter into a paste, add to broth stirring until thickened. Add cream and shelled oysters and heat until almost boiling. Serve at once.

✳

## PINON SOUP

1 lb. pinon nuts                    1 quart milk
2 cup chicken broth                 5 scallions, sliced
1/4 tsp. coriander                  4 dried mint leaves
1/4 tsp. pepper                     chives, minced

Heat all ingredients except chives together until mixture simmers. Simmer for 20 minutes. Puree in blender until smooth. Reheat and garnish with chives. Soup may be served hot or cold.

## PINON AND
## MINT SOUP

6 cup beef consomme          1/2 cup pinon nuts
2 cans chick-peas            2 stalks mint

Combine all ingredients except mint. Bring to a boil and simmer 15 minutes. Turn off heat, add mint, steep 1 minutes and serve.

## DRIED CORN

12 ears corn

Carefully peel back husks, leaving them attached at base. Clean corn, removing silks. Fold husks back into position. Place on wire rack in large shallow baking pan allowing space between ears so air can circulate. Bake at 325 for 1 1/2 hours. Cool, strip back husks and hang by husks in a dry place until kernels are dry (about a week).

## FRUIT ROLLS

Peaches, pears, apricots, or berries may be used. Wash and pit or seed fruit, mash into a puree. Spread on cookie sheets to an even 1/inch thickness. Dry in hot sun for 8 to 10 hours or on a shelf in a warm place for 1 to 2 weeks or oven fry at 150 F. for 4 to 5 hours. Dry until puree is firm and edges can be lifted easily. Peel from cookie sheets while still warm and roll into scrolls. Dry in paper or cloth bags for 4 to 5 days and then store in airtight containers.

## JUNIPER TEA

*20 tender young sprigs of juniper washed*
*2 quarts water*

Place the juniper sprigs and water in a large saucepan, bring to a boil, cover, reduce heat, and let simmer for 10 minutes. Turn heat off and let tea steep for 10 minutes. Strain and serve.

# ZUNIGREEN
# CHILI STEW

3 lbs. Boned lamb cut into 1 1/2" cubes
1 medium red chili pepper, crushed

flour                                             1 tbsp. salt

2 tbsp. cooking oil          2 garlic cloves, peeled and crushed

1/4 tsp. ground black pepper                 2 tsp. oregano

6 dried juniper berries, crushed        1/2 cup minced parsley

5 1/2 cups canned hominy (include liquid)      1 quart water

2 onions, peeled and chopped

6 green peppers, cored and quartered

Dust lamb cubes with flour

Brown lamb slowly on all sides in the cooking oil in a large heavy skillet. As the meat browns, add the black pepper and crushed juniper berries.

Transfer meat to paper toweling to drain. In the same kettle, saute the onions slowly until golden. Return meat to kettle.

Mix in the remaining ingredients, cover, and simmer for 1 1/2 hours, stirring occasionally.

## BEAN MOLD

1/2 lb. dry pea beans

2 strips bacon, diced and rendered
(reserve drippings)

1/2 cup corn meal

1 tsp. salt

1/8 tsp. ground pepper

1/2 tsp. paprika

4 dashes tabasco Sauce

    Soak and cook beans according to package directions, reserving 2 cups of their cooking water. If there are not 2 cups, add enough water to complete the measure.

    Mash the beans and mix with the bacon drippings, and corn meal.

    Bring the 2 cups of water to boil, add the bean mixture along with the salt.

✳

## BAKEDTURNIPS

1 1/2 lbs. small white turnips

1/4 cup butter margarine

1/2 tsp. salt

1/4 tsp. coarse ground pepper

    Wash turnips well and trim off stems. Parboil for 20 to 30 minutes or until fork will just pierce them.

    Place in a shallow baking dish, pour the remaining ingredients, which have been mixed over the turnips. Bake at 350 F for 45 minutes

**243.**

# DRIED CORN

## SOUP

1 ear dried corn, removed from the cob          7 cups water
1 (2"x1") strip fat back, sliced          5 oz. dried beef
1/8 tsp. fresh ground pepper

Soak the corn in 2 cups water for 48 hours.

Place the corn and its soaking water in a large saucepan. Add the remaining water and the fat back, and simmer, covered for about 3 hours and 50 minutes or until the corn is tender but not soft.

Mix in the dried beef and pepper, and simmer, stirring, for 10 minutes more. Serve hot.

# EGGS AND WILD ONIONS

5 slices bacon, cut into julienne strips
1 1/2 tbsp. minced parsley

8 eggs, slightly beaten          1 1/2 tsp. salt
1/2 cup minced scallions or chives     1/2 tsp. fresh ground pepper

Brown the bacon in a large heavy skillet

Add eggs, scallions, parsley, salt and pepper, and scramble gently.

Serve at once.

# 244.
# FRIED CUCUMBERS

*4 large cucumbers washed and cut into slices 1/8" thick*
*Salt and coarsely ground pepper to taste*
*season flour for dusting*
*Oil or vegetable shortening for frying*

Spread cucumber slices between layers of paper towelling to dry. Let stand for about an hour.

Remove towelling and season slices with salt and pepper.

Dip slices on flour and coat both sides lightly.

Fry quickly in deep fat until slices are golden brown on each side.

Drain on paper towelling and serve at once.

✻

# HOMINY SOUP

*1/4 lb. salt pork, sliced about 1/4" thick*
*1 medium onion, peeled and sliced thin*
*2 (1 lb. 13 oz.) cans hominy, drained*      *1 quart buttermilk*
*1/2 teaspoon salt*      *1/4 tsp. fresh ground pepper*

Render the salt pork thoroughly in a large, heavy kettle. Drain off drippings.

Add the onion to the kettle , and saute slowly until golden and transparent.

Mix in hominy, and heat gently, stirring, for about 5 minutes.

Add buttermilk, salt, and pepper, and heat very slowly (do not allow to simmer) for about 5 minutes. This soup should be served warm, not hot.

# BAKED HOMINY

*4 cucumbers, peeled and quartered lengthwise*
*2 tbsp. butter or margarine*
*1 tsp. salt*        *1 tsp. dill seed, crushed*
*1/4 tsp. fresh ground pepper*

Place a layer of cucumbers in the bottom of an 8"x8"x4" baking dish and dot with half of the butter or margarine.

Mix together the seasonings, and sprinkle half over the layer of cucumbers.

Add a second layer of cucumbers, dot with butter, and sprinkle with remaining seasonings.

Bake uncovered, in a hot oven, 400 F for 1 hour.  Stir cucumber lightly once, pushing the top layer to the bottom and lifting the bottom cucumbers to the top.  Serve hot.

# BEAN CAKE

*1/2 lb. pea beans, washed, soaked*    *1 tsp. baking powder*
*and cooked by pkg. directions*    *1/8 tsp. fresh ground powder*
*1 cup corn meal*        *1 cup milk*
*1 cup flour*        *2 eggs, lightly beaten*
*2 tsp. salt*        *2 tbsp. cooking oil*

Drain the beans thoroughly, and cool to room temperature.

Sift together the corn meal, flour, salt, baking powder, and pepper. Mix together the milk and eggs, and then stir them into the sifted dry ingredients.

Fold in the beans.  Heat the oil in a pan and add to the cake mixture.  Place in a cake pan and bake at 350 F., for 40 minutes.  Serve hot.

# NUTS AND BERRIES
# INFORMATION AND RECIPES

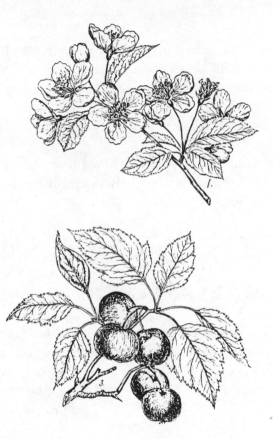

## CRABAPPLE

To be picked in the fall, after the first frost.

WHITE BLOSSOMS: On tree turn to fruit of yellow-green.

HOPA CRABAPPLE: Pink apple blossoms followed by fruit red all the way through. All recipes use the crabapple differently, so follow directions in recipe being used. Make sure to always wash and remove blossoms and stems. Cut out any bruised or wormy parts.

## CRANBERRIES

Gather this fruit in October. Cranberries will stay on stem all winter long. The fruit is scarlet red; the stems are trailing and wiry.

There are many ways to use cranberries and they will keep for months and months. Wash well in cold water 2 or 3 times. Pack in sterilized jars and refrigerate. To freeze; lay out on tray and freeze for about 2 hours. When frozen, place in containers or in freezer bags. When needed, rinse out in cold water and use in any recipe calling for fresh cranberries.

## ELDERBERRIES

Pick in July to the middle of August. The berries are magenta-purple, almost black in color and grow in a single cluster. During June and July, clusters of tiny, creamy-white flowers bloom. these flowers are called "Elderblow". Both the berries and the flowers are edible. The Indians used the stems as well. They made maple spiles, pea-shooters, and whistles with them.

The berries are best when dried. Excellent for use in pies, muffins, sauces and juices. Always stew berries with a little sugar first; strain, and use in recipe. Elderberry has little acid and so is best mixed with other fruit.

When using elderblow, simple remove any coarse stems and rinse.

## HUCKLEBERRIES & BLUEBERRIES

HUCKLEBERRY: Is smaller and darker in color than the blueberry and has a hard seedlike berry. Gather these in July and August.

BLUEBERRY: These are gather in July and August also. The fruits are blue-black in color, with a waxy bloom and many soft seeds.

PREPARATION: Simply pick through berries, removing all smashed or green berries. Place in pot filled with water and skim off whatever floats to the top.

## WILD RASPBERRIES

Pick in July or early August. The fruits are red (sometimes yellow) and juicy. Each is an aggregate of several tiny individual fruits. When the berries are ripe, they separate easily from the white central receptacle and fall off in a typical thimble form. Sort through berries carefully, removing any bruised or wormy fruit. Wash in cold water; drain; and let dry. The fruit is picked in the month of August.

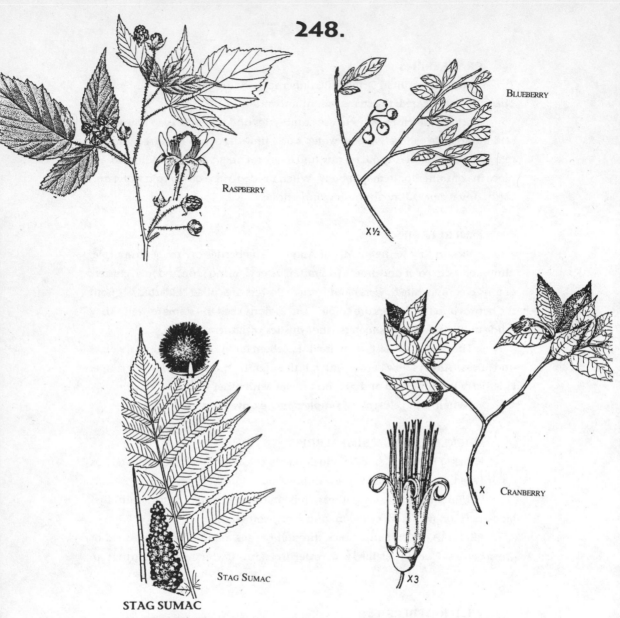

RASPBERRY

BLUEBERRY

X ½

STAG SUMAC

X

CRANBERRY

X3

## STAG SUMAC

EDIBLE BERRIES:  Are hard and bright red in color, covered with tiny hairs.

POISONOUS BERRIES:  Are white in color and hang loosely.

Sumacs are usually found in the same areas as the elderberry.  In recipes they complement other, less acidic, fruits such as the elderberry.

## ACORNS

Acorns are gathered in the fall. Roasted and salted acorns have a taste crossed between sunflowers seeds and popcorn.

**RED OAKS:** Bitter Acorns - Oval -shaped with wooly hairs lining the cup. These acorns will remain on the trees throughout the winter months. To remove the bitterness; first shell, then boil the kernels for 2 hours or more changing the water each time it becomes tea colored. Use only boiling water for the changes so as not to interrupt the boiling procedure. Continue until water remains clear and nut is chocolate brown in color.

**WHITE OAKS:** Sweet Acorns - Oval-shaped with smooth inner wall of cup. Needs only to be shelled and roasted.

SUGGESTIONS: Dip dried acorns in clarified sugar; serve. Ground meal can be used as a substitute for conventional flour in baking. Good as a soup thickener. Roasted acorns are also a popular coffee substitute.

✳

## BLACK WALNUTS

Gather in the fall. Fruit is globular-shaped and have fleshly yellow-green husks with a hard black nut inside. Its best to wear gloves when gathering, as shells will discolor your hands. Coloring makes excellent dye which is almost impossible to remove. The best way to break the husk and shell is with a hammer.

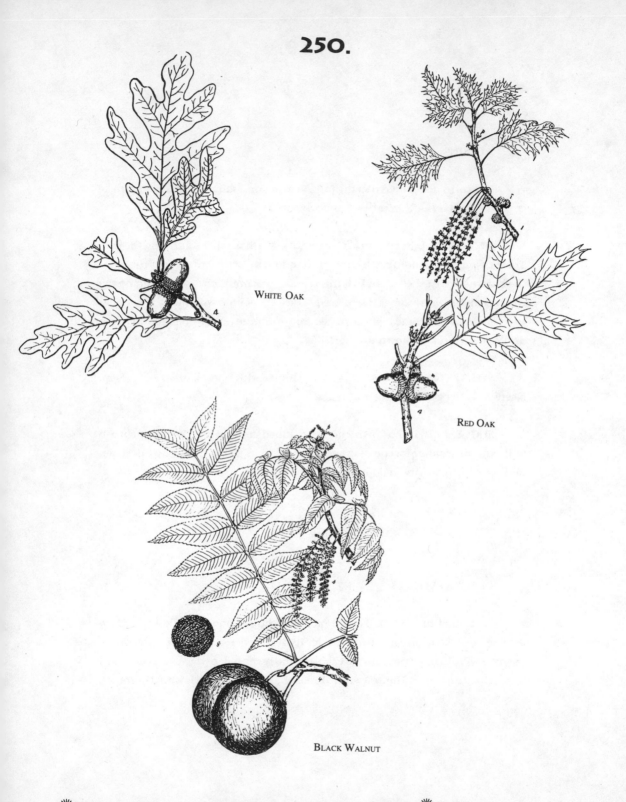

White Oak

Red Oak

Black Walnut

## BUTTERNUTS

Butternuts should be gathered in the fall. Also referred to as the "White Walnut". The fruit is elliptical in shape and the husk is a sticky, and yellowy-green. The kernel is even harder to extract than that of the walnut. You can accomplish this only by repeated blows from a hammer. Use these kernels in place of walnuts. Roast kernels in a moderate oven of about 300 F, until dried. Leave whole; chopped, or pulverized. Store in glass containers and seal tightly.

## HAZELNUTS

Pick in the fall after the first frost. Leaves appear alternately on the branches; never in pairs and are oval shaped and sharply toothed. Nuts have a stinging, tubular husk covering them. To remove skins, spread on baking pan and heat in 325 F oven for 30 minutes, cool; then skins should rub off easily.

## CHESTNUTS

Chestnut trees are very scarce today. The fruit is dark brown with a burred, pickly shell. Found in clusters of 2 to 6 fruit. Roast over open fire for about 10 minutes, then remove from shells. An alternate method is to roast in the oven for about 1 hour on a salted tray; remove from shell and then pour melted butter over the top.

## MAPLE SYRUP

Trees should be tapped early in the spring. Good syrup can be obtained from all maples but the sugar maple is the most common. To tap the maple tree for sap, make a V - shaped groove through the bark with a a knife. Use a spile made from a tin can lid, a piece of birchbark, or elderberry stems, and insert them into the incision to allow the sap to drain out. A delicious syrup can be made by boiling the sap for about 2 hours, depending on preferred texture and consistency. An average sized tree will yield approximately 1 gallon of syrup per year. Two taps or spiles can be put into most trees.

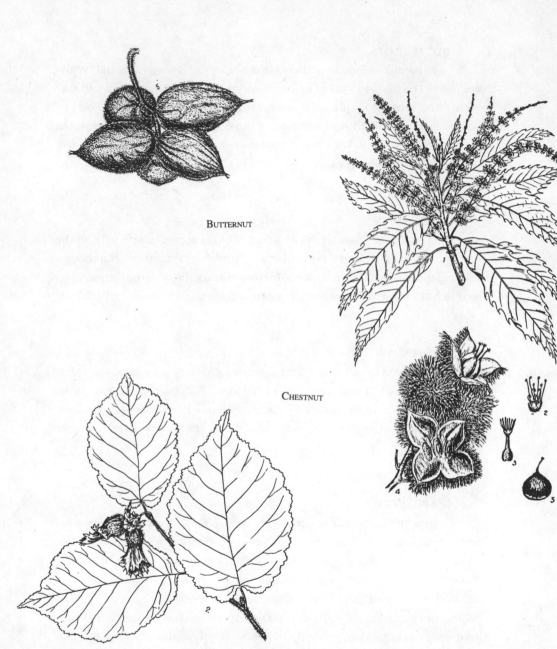

BUTTERNUT

CHESTNUT

HAZELNUT

# WILD
# RASPBERRY CAKE

| | |
|---|---|
| 1 3/4 cups flour | 1 tsp. baking soda (dissolved in 1/2 cup milk) |
| 1/2 tsp. salt | 2 eggs, slightly beaten |
| 1 cup white sugar | 3/4 cup shortening |
| 1 cup raspberries | 1 tsp. cinnamon |

Sift together, flour, salt, sugar, cinnamon. Cut in shortening. Then mix in soda, eggs and raspberries. Pour into a greased pan and bake at 325 F for 1 hour.

# BLUEBERRY
# ORANGE LOAF

| | |
|---|---|
| 1/2 tsp. baking soda | 1/4 cup orange juice |
| 2 tsp. baking powder | 1/4 cup melted butter |
| 2 cups all purpose flour | 3/4 cups milk |
| 3/4 cup sugar | 1 egg, beaten |
| 3/4 tsp. salt | 1 cup blueberries |
| 1 tbsp. grated orange rind | 1/2 cup chopped nuts |

Sift together first 5 ingredients into a bowl. In a separate bowl combine the next five ingredients and stir into the flour mixture. Beat well. Grease a 9x4x3 inch loaf pan and spread with 1/3 of the batter. Sprinkle 1/2 the blueberries and nuts. Add 1/3 more batter then, the remaining blueberries and nuts. Add rest of batter. Bake at 350 F for 50 minutes. Add frosting if desired when cool.

# BLUEBERRY CAKE

1/2 cup butter or margarine    1 cup + 1 tbsp. white sugar
1/4 tsp. salt                              1 tsp. vanilla
2 eggs, separated                    1 1/2 cups + 1 tbsp. flour
1 tsp. baking powder                  1/3 cup milk
            1 1/2 cups blueberries

Cream butter and 3/4 cup sugar. Add salt and vanilla. Add egg yolks. Beat until creamy. Combine 1 1/2 cups flour and baking powder. Add alternately with milk to egg mixture. Beat egg whites until soft adding 1/4 cup sugar. Beat until stiff. Coat berries with 1 tbsp. flour and add to batter. Fold in egg whites. Pour into 8 inch greased cake pan. Sprinkle on top 1 tbsp. sugar. Bake at 350 F for 50 minutes, or until toothpick inserted into the center of cake comes out clean.

# BAKED RHUBARB
# AND STRAWBERRIES

1/2 lb. rhubarb
1/2 lb. strawberries
1 cup brown sugar

Wash and cut rhubarb in 2 inch cubes. Add strawberries, and sugar and mix with rhubarb. Place mixture in baking dish, and cover and bake at 350 F for 35 to 45 minutes.

# STRAWBERRIES
# AND HONEY

*1 quart wild strawberries*       *6 oz. cream cheese*
*1/2 cup honey*                   *1 cup sour cream*
*2 tbsp. white wine*

Combine cheese, honey and sour cream until perfectly smooth. Stir in wine.  Place strawberries on a serving dish and spoon honey sauce over them.

# SIMMERED GOOSEBERRIES

*1 quart gooseberries*
*1 1/2 cups water*
*1 1/2 cups sugar*

Wash and remove the blossoms.  Pick off stems and remove any berries that are soft. Put sugar and water in a saucepan and bring to a boil. Then add berries and simmer till berries are cooked through, stirring occasionally. Do not let berries get soft and mushy. Just before the berries are cooked, add the sugar.

# PUMPKIN SOUP

1 (1 lb. 13 oz.) can water-packed pumpkin puree
1/2 tsp. powdered marjoram

| | |
|---|---|
| 1 quart milk | dash fresh ground pepper |
| 2 tbsp. butter or margarine | 1/4 tsp. cinnamon |
| 2 tbsp. honey | 1/4 tsp. mace |

2 tbsp. maple syrup or light brown sugar
1 tsp. salt
juice of 1 orange

Heat pumpkin puree, milk, butter, and honey together slowly in a large saucepan, stirring. Combine maple sugar, marjoram, pepper, cinnamon, mace, and salt, stir into pumpkin-milk mixture. Heat slowly, stirring to simmering point. Do not boil Add the orange juice, a little at a time, stirring constantly. Serve hot.

❋

# CHERRY BALLS

1 lb. dried choke cherries
1 cup tallow or shortening
1 cup sugar

Grind up wild choke cherries. Add tallow or shortening; then add the sugar. Form into balls the size of a golf ball. This was always a treat for the Sioux children. With the above instructions for preparation you may substitute pounded dried beef or venison in place of the choke cherries.

# PLAINS INDIAN DESSERT

Bring whole wild choke cherries to a boil; just covering them with water. Mash gently with potato masher. Strain juice from choke cherries into a pan; add one cup sugar for each pint of juice and two tablespoons of cornstarch.

Heat and stir until thickness of custard. Serve in individual bowls, either warm or cold. Plums or other wild fruit may be used instead of choke cherries.

# CHERRY WOZAPI (DESSERT)

*6 patties of dried cherries (soak cherries*
*for 1 hour until soft)*

*1 cup sugar*
*1/2 cup flour*
*bits of tallow for flavoring*

Boil the cherry patties in water for 2 hours. Drain the liquid and use for the sauce. Mix the white sauce and gradually add to the cherry liquid. Stir carefully. Add the tallow and sugar. Stir well until it reaches a thick consistency, when it is ready to serve.

## MAPLE SYRUP

The Indians were the first people to make maple syrup and sugar. A tomahawk was used to make a slant cut into a tree. They drove a flat piece of wood into the lower end of the cut. The sap ran along this piece of wood and into a birchbark dish.

Women and girls poured this sap into birchbark pails and carried it to the boiling place.

The Indians made kettles of green birchbark because the green bark would not burn for a long time.

During the boiling process, the water evaporated and the maple syrup remained.

If boiled long enough, the maple syrup will turn into sugar.

## ACORN MEAL

Make meal by grinding dry, raw acorn kernels. Mix with boiling water and press out liquid through a cheesecloth. With very bitter acorns, repeat this process several times. then spread meal on a tray and thoroughly dry in oven at 250 F.

This meal will cake during the drying process. Regrind using a food chopper. Then, seal in containers, preferably glass jars.

## ACORN BREAD

| | |
|---|---|
| 1 cup acorn meal | 3 tbsp. sugar |
| 1 cup flour | 1 egg, beaten |
| 2 tbsp. baking powder | 1 cup milk |
| 1/2 tsp. salt | 3 tbsp. oil |

Sift together, acorn meal, white flour, baking powder, salt and sugar. In separate bowl, mix together egg, milk and oil. Combine dry ingredients and liquid ingredients. Stir just enough to moisten dry ingredients. Pour into a greased pan and bake at 400 F for 30 minutes.

※

## ACORN PANCAKES

| | |
|---|---|
| 1 cup acorn meal | 3 tbsp. sugar |
| 1 cup flour | 2 eggs, beaten |
| 2 tbsp. baking powder | 1 1/2 cups milk |
| 1 tsp. salt | 3 tbsp. oil |

Sift together dry ingredients. In separate bowl mix together eggs, milk and oil. Then, combine dry ingredients with liquid mixture. Spread batter thinly on a hot griddle. When edges begin to bubble, flip and brown on other side. Serve with maple syrup or jelly.

## BUTTERNUT SAUCE

2 cups butternut, shelled          salt and pepper to taste
1/2 cup olive oil                  2 tsp. parsley
juice of 1/2 lemon                 1 tsp. tarragon

Blend parsley, tarragon and butternuts in a blender. Add olive oil, seasonings and lemon juice. Blend thoroughly on medium speed. This sauce is a nice dip for cold fish.

## MAPLE NUTS

8 oz. grated maple sugar          3 oz. walnuts or acorns
6 oz. water                       14 oz. dried prunes (stoned)
          4 oz. broken wild hazelnuts

Place maple sugar and water in a large saucepan. Heat slowly without stirring. Remove from heat, drop walnuts in this hot syrup and stir to be sure all parts will be sugared. then drop alternately, hazelnuts and prunes and stir well. Remove with a skimming ladle and cool.

## BLACK WALNUT SOUFFLE

1 cup walnuts or butternuts, finely chopped          1/4 lb. butter
1/2 cup sugar                                        1/2 cup cream
                    6 eggs, separated

   In a bowl, cream butter.  Add egg yolks, one at a time, beating
between each addition. Add cream, sugar and nuts, beating continu-
ously. Whip egg whites stiff and fold them into the creamy mixture. Pour
into a greased souffle dish and bake at 375 F for 1 hour.

## BUTTERNUT CAKE

1 1/2 cups sugar                                          3 eggs
1/2 cup butter, melted                           2 tsp. cream of tartar
1/2 cup milk                                       1 tsp. baking soda
                    2 cups flour

### FILLING:

              2 cups butternuts, pulverized
      1 tbsp. cornstarch, mixed with 2 tbsp. cold milk
1 cup sweet corn                                     1 tbsp. sugar

Combine flour, soda, cream of tartar and sugar. Mix in butter, eggs and milk. Grease pans and pour the batter in. Bake at 350 F for 35 to 45 minutes in 2 (8 inch) round pans.

To make filling; let cream come to a boil, then stir in cornstarch and sugar. Bring to a boil again and remove from stove. Stir in the butternuts. When partially cooled, spread between the 2 layers.

# CHESTNUT

# SOUP

| | |
|---|---|
| 1 lb. prepared chestnuts | pepper |
| 2 celery stalks and leaves | 2 cups chicken broth |
| 1 tsp. parsley | 1/2 cup cream |
| 1 tsp. thyme | 3 tsp. Sherry |
| salt | whipped cream |

Tie herbs together in a cheesecloth bag. In a soup kettle combine chestnuts, herbs and seasoning and cover with boiling water. Simmer until chestnuts are soft. Remove herbs and either sieve the soup or put it into a blender. Add chicken broth and cream and bring to a boil. Add Sherry and serve at once with salted whipped cream.

# CHESTNUTS
# AND BACON

*12 chestnuts*
*12 strips of bacon*

Remove shells and skins of the chestnuts. Cover with boiling water and simmer until tender. Drain. Fasten bacon strips around chestnuts with toothpicks. Put under boiler until bacon is crisp.

# HAZELNUT
# CAKES

*2 cups hazelnuts, unroasted*      *1 tsp. salt*
*2 cups water*      *1/4 cup vegetable oil*
*1/3 cup cornmeal*

Grind nuts and mix with water in a saucepan. Heat to boiling; reduce heat and simmer for 30 minutes, stirring frequently. Mix in cornmeal and slat and let stand for 20 minutes or until it thickens. Drop the nut batter with a large spoon on greased grill. When browned on one side flip it over and brown the other side. Serve with butter and honey or maple syrup.

# SPICED

# CRABAPPLES

crabapples
1 quart vinegar
4 cups sugar

1 tbsp. stick cinnamon
1 tbsp. whole cloves
1 tbsp. mace

1 tbsp. allspice

Wash and remove blossom end of firm crabapples. Do not peel. Mix vinegar, sugar and spices. Boil until syrup coats a spoon. Add apples, reheat mixture slowly to avoid bursting the skins and simmer until apples are tender. Pack into clean sterile hot jars. Cover with hot syrup and seal.

# CHAPTER · NINE ·
# HOMEMADE WINES
# HERBAL REMEDIES

## DANDELION WINE

4 quarts dandelion blossoms

4 quarts water

3 lbs. sugar

3 lemons, sliced

1 yeast cake

Combine blossoms & water in a crock and let stand covered for nine days. Squeeze out the blossoms and strain juice. Add sugar, lemons and yeast cake and let stand for another nine days.

Strain liquid and put it in a jug, leaving the cork out until fermentation ceases. Then cork it!

✳

## BEETROOT WINE

6 lbs. beets

1 gallon water

few grains of rice

3 lbs. sugar, white

2 lbs. seedless raisins

juice of 2 lemons

1 oz. yeast

1 slice of toast

### DIRECTIONS

Wash beets and cut into small pieces. Boil gently in one gallon of water for two hours. Strain and pour into a large crock. Add raisins, lemons and rice, then stir in sugar until completely dissolved.

Spread yeast on one side of toast and place yeast-side down on the liquid. Cover and let stand 10 to 12 days, stirring three times daily. Strain and bottle.

# WILD RICE WINE

3 lbs. wild rice, cleaned

3 lbs. sugar

1 gallon warm water

1 lemon

1 oz. cherry wine yeast

pinch of isinglass (clearing agent)

1 lb raisins, ground or chopped fine

Put the rice and sugar in a large bowl and cover with warm water. Mix in raisins. Squeeze the juice from one lemon and add to the mixture. Make sure the temperature of the water is not over 65 F., then sprinkle the yeast and isinglass over the top. Cover and allow to ferment for nine days, stirring frequently for the first three days. After nine days, strain through a paper-filtered, fine sieve.

Transfer the liquid into gallon fermenting jars. Put on the fermentation locks and let stand. When the wine is completely clear, bottle and store. The wine is harsh and strong but the taste will improve greatly with age.

# HERBAL AND NATURAL
# REMEDIES

Natural medicines are from many of the trees and bark,   plants and berries found around your home, campsites, along the roads, and in the woods.  These are not magic medicines and all should be investigated by you, your  doctor, and the government before you   use any home-made remedies.  Then and only then, should you try them, but remember people are individuals and these remedies may affect you differently. Use at your own risk.

We will include a large selection of these in our next book.

Here are three common wild plant cures.

## FOR EXTERNAL SWELLING:

Pulverize the fresh PIPSISSWEA plant and apply moist to the swelling.

## FOR SORE THROAT:

Toast JUNIPER twigs and make a hot pack out of a piece of leather. Place it on the throat.

## TOOTHACHE:

Crush the bark of the BUTTERNUT TREE and apply to the sore tooth.

# · CHAPTER TEN ·
# SMOKING AND CURING OF FISH AND GAME

Lacking refrigeration, Native Indians developed many ways of preserving foods. Meat and seafood were smoked or dried, vegetables and fruits were dried. Often caches of this preserved food were stored in the trees under cedar bark so hunters did not have to carry large supplies of food with them on their travels. The Blackfeet also pickled their meat in brine in a process similar to modern corned beef.

Fruits and vegetables were commonly sun-dried. In the damper climates such as that of the Northwest, some tribes used drying racks of woven cedar mats placed over open fires. Fruits and berries are mashed into a pulp and spread thinly over sheets to make fruit leathers or dried in brick form. Combinations of various fruits and berries in season produce delicious flavor variations.

Dried meat and fruits were rehydrated for use in the winter. You may find this interesting to try, as the flavor is different than the same recipe using fresh ingredients.

Cold-smoked meat keeps much longer than cooked smoking where the temperatures are higher 150-200 F. Indians cold-smoked meat by hanging high over the cooking fire for about a week.

For smoking game meat the best woods are mesquite, hickory, oak and citrus. Fish taste best when cooked over a buttonwood, mangorve or baywood fire.

In addition to the recipes that follow, please see the following recipes and pages:

| | |
|---|---|
| *Pickled Venison Heart* | *(page 11)* |
| *Pemmican recipes* | *(page 42)* |
| *Making Jerky* | *(page 44)* |
| *Dried Corn* | *(page 239)* |
| *Fruit Rolls* | *(page 240)* |

## CURED VENISON

3 lbs. salt
5 tbsp. pepper

4 tbsp. cinnamon
4 tbsp. allspice

Venison

Cut meat into strips 12 inches long, two inches thick and four inches wide. Remove all membranes so curing mixture will adhere to moist meat. Mix dry ingredients thoroughly and rub well into every surface of meat, dust on extra as well. Thread each strip on a string and hang in a dry cool place out of sun and artificial heat. Meat needs to be hung for approximately a month before eating.

# SMOKED HERRING

1 lb. coarse salt
1 tbsp. salt, pepper
1 tbsp. cloves, crushed
2 tbsp. onions, minced

2 cups brown sugar
2 tbsp. garlic, minced
1 tbsp. bay leaves, crushed
2 lbs. herring

Make a paste of all ingredients except herring. Clean and gut herring. Coat herring with paste and cure for seven days in refrigerator. Reapply mixture as needed so fish remains coated. After seven days, rinse and hang thoroughly to dry. Cold smoke over fire. For home smokers, smoke at 70-85 for seven days.

# SMOKE CURED EGGS

Remove the egg sack from salmon, making sure not to put any holes in it. Tie ends with string and hang at the side of the fire. Smoke from the fire will dry and cure it in about four days. When done, it is firm and dry inside and out. It looks and taste like sausage.

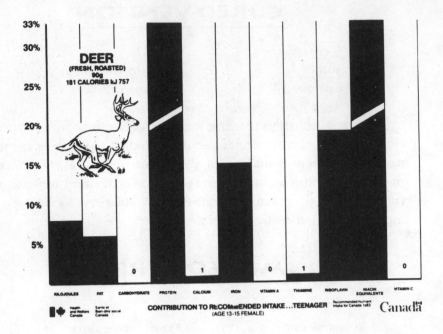

**DEER**
(FRESH, ROASTED)
90g
181 CALORIES kJ 757

| KILOJOULES | FAT | CARBOHYDRATE | PROTEIN | CALCIUM | IRON | VITAMIN A | THIAMINE | RIBOFLAVIN | NIACIN EQUIVALENTS | VITAMIN C |
|---|---|---|---|---|---|---|---|---|---|---|
| | | 0 | | 1 | | 0 | 1 | | | 0 |

**CONTRIBUTION TO RECOMMENDED INTAKE...TEENAGER**
(AGE 13-15 FEMALE)

Health and Welfare Canada   Santé et Bien-être social Canada   Recommended Nutrient Intake for Canada 1983   Canadä

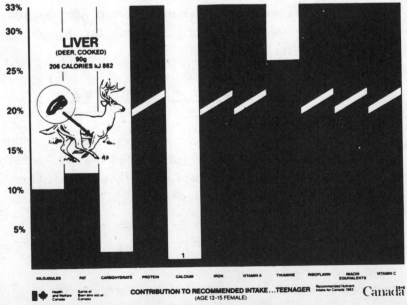

**LIVER**
(DEER, COOKED)
90g
206 CALORIES kJ 862

| KILOJOULES | FAT | CARBOHYDRATE | PROTEIN | CALCIUM | IRON | VITAMIN A | THIAMINE | RIBOFLAVIN | NIACIN EQUIVALENTS | VITAMIN C |
|---|---|---|---|---|---|---|---|---|---|---|
| | | | | 1 | | | | | | |

**CONTRIBUTION TO RECOMMENDED INTAKE...TEENAGER**
(AGE 13-15 FEMALE)

Health and Welfare Canada   Santé et Bien-être social Canada   Recommended Nutrient Intake for Canada 1983   Canadä

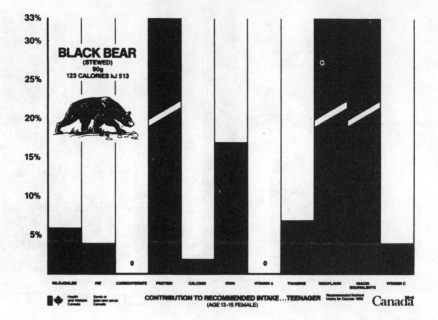

**BLACK BEAR**
(STEWED)
90g
123 CALORIES kJ 513

33%
30%
25%
20%
15%
10%
5%

0                    0

KILOJOULES    FAT    CARBOHYDRATE    PROTEIN    CALCIUM    IRON    VITAMIN A    THIAMINE    RIBOFLAVIN    NIACIN EQUIVALENTS    VITAMIN C

Health and Welfare Canada / Santé et Bien-être social Canada

**CONTRIBUTION TO RECOMMENDED INTAKE...TEENAGER**
(AGE 13-15 FEMALE)

Recommended Nutrient Intake for Canada 1983

Canadä

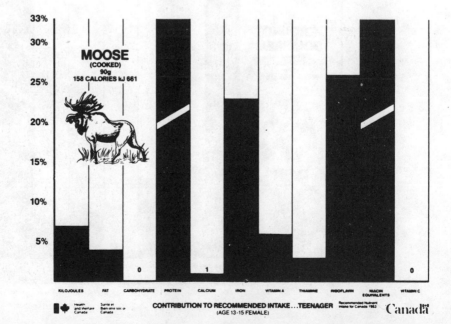

**MOOSE**
(COOKED)
90g
158 CALORIES kJ 661

33%
30%
25%
20%
15%
10%
5%

0            1                            0

KILOJOULES    FAT    CARBOHYDRATE    PROTEIN    CALCIUM    IRON    VITAMIN A    THIAMINE    RIBOFLAVIN    NIACIN EQUIVALENTS    VITAMIN C

Health and Welfare Canada / Santé et Bien-être social Canada

**CONTRIBUTION TO RECOMMENDED INTAKE...TEENAGER**
(AGE 13-15 FEMALE)

Recommended Nutrient Intake for Canada 1983

Canadä

**272.**

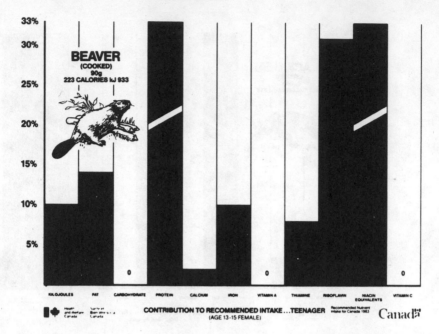

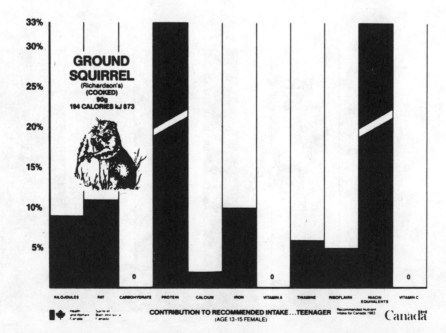

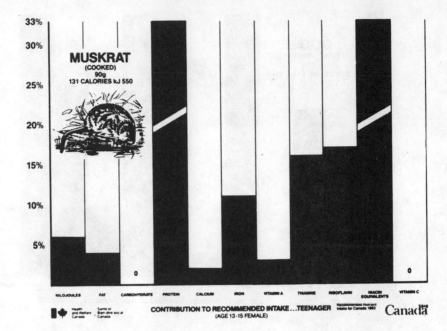

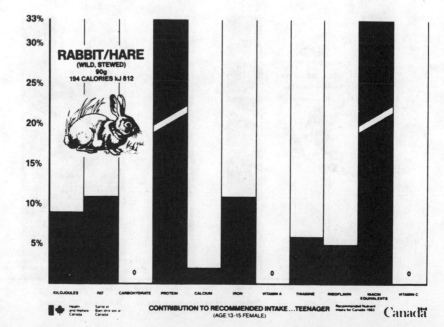

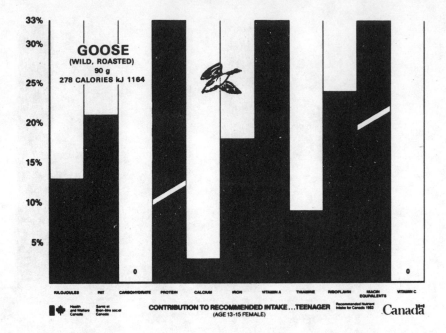

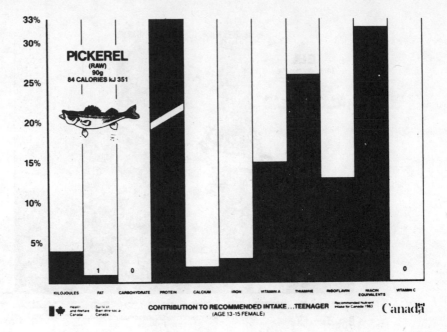

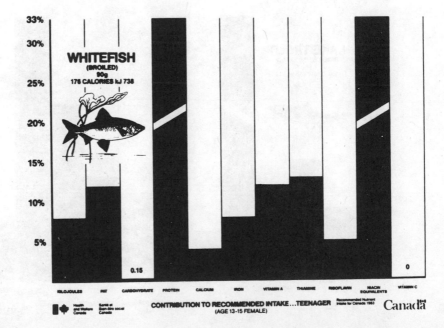

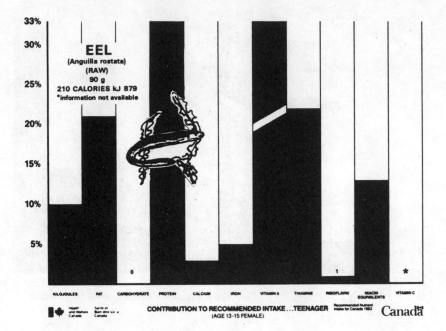

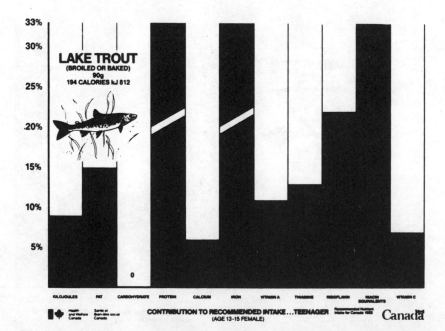

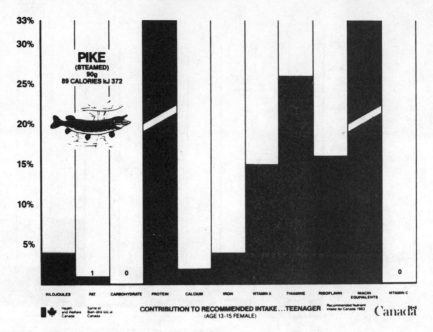

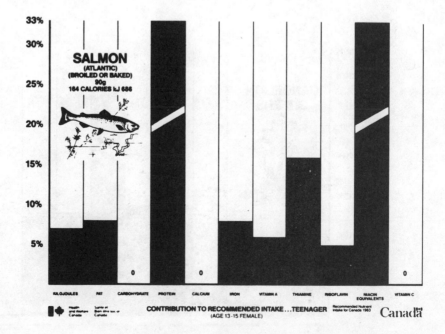

# 278.

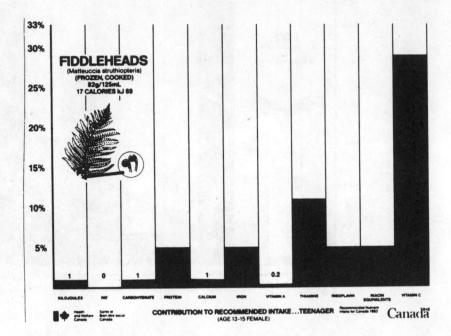

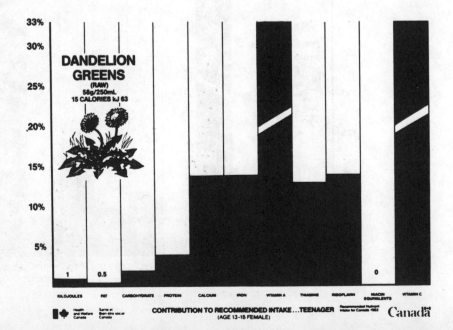

# 279.

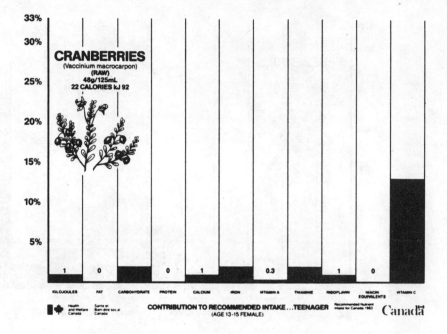

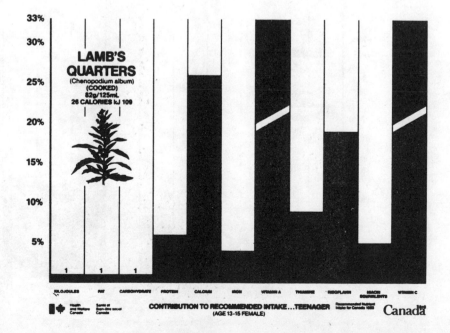

# 280.

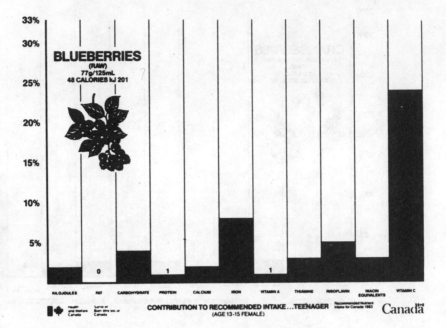

33%
30%
25%
20%
15%
10%
5%

**BLUEBERRIES**
(RAW)
77g/125mL
48 CALORIES kJ 201

0                    1                    1

KILOJOULES  FAT  CARBOHYDRATE  PROTEIN  CALCIUM  IRON  VITAMIN A  THIAMINE  RIBOFLAVIN  NIACIN EQUIVALENTS  VITAMIN C

Health and Welfare Canada    Santé et Bien-être social Canada    **CONTRIBUTION TO RECOMMENDED INTAKE...TEENAGER**  Recommended Nutrient Intake for Canada 1983    Canada
(AGE 13-15 FEMALE)

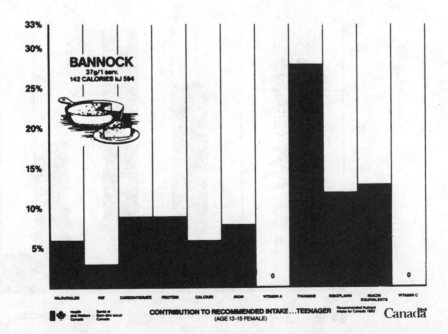

33%
30%
25%
20%
15%
10%
5%

**BANNOCK**
37g/1 serv.
142 CALORIES kJ 594

0                                        0

KILOJOULES  FAT  CARBOHYDRATE  PROTEIN  CALCIUM  IRON  VITAMIN A  THIAMINE  RIBOFLAVIN  NIACIN EQUIVALENTS  VITAMIN C

Health and Welfare Canada    Santé et Bien-être social Canada    **CONTRIBUTION TO RECOMMENDED INTAKE...TEENAGER**  Recommended Nutrient Intake for Canada 1983    Canada
(AGE 13-15 FEMALE)

# 281.

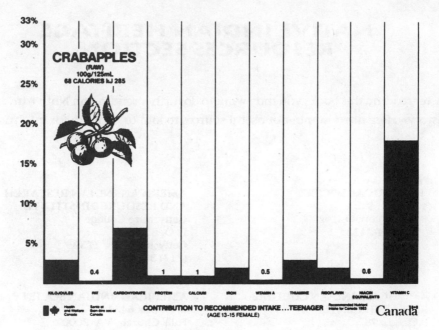

**CRABAPPLES**
(RAW)
100g/125mL
68 CALORIES kJ 285

| | | | | | | | | | | |
|---|---|---|---|---|---|---|---|---|---|---|
| KILOJOULES | FAT | CARBOHYDRATE | PROTEIN | CALCIUM | IRON | VITAMIN A | THIAMINE | RIBOFLAVIN | NIACIN EQUIVALENTS | VITAMIN C |
| | 0.4 | | 1 | 1 | | 0.5 | | | 0.6 | |

Health and Welfare Canada   Santé et Bien-être social Canada

**CONTRIBUTION TO RECOMMENDED INTAKE...TEENAGER**
(AGE 13-15 FEMALE)

Recommended Nutrient Intake for Canada 1983

Canada

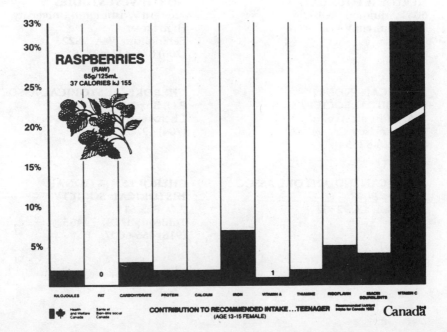

**RASPBERRIES**
(RAW)
65g/125mL
37 CALORIES kJ 155

| | | | | | | | | | | |
|---|---|---|---|---|---|---|---|---|---|---|
| KILOJOULES | FAT | CARBOHYDRATE | PROTEIN | CALCIUM | IRON | VITAMIN A | THIAMINE | RIBOFLAVIN | NIACIN EQUIVALENTS | VITAMIN C |
| | 0 | | | | | 1 | | | | |

Health and Welfare Canada   Santé et Bien-être social Canada

**CONTRIBUTION TO RECOMMENDED INTAKE...TEENAGER**
(AGE 13-15 FEMALE)

Recommended Nutrient Intake for Canada 1983

Canada

# NATIVE INDIAN HERITAGE
# RESOURCES SECTION

After reading this book , you may want to do further reading on Native traditions and history.  Here are a number of useful sources to join or  write to for information:

**AMERICAN
 HISTORICAL SOCIETY**
400 A St., S.E.
Washington, D.C.  20003
(202) 544-2422

**AMERICAN  INDIAN CULTURE
RESEARCH CENTER**
P.O. Box 98
Blue Cloud Abbey
Marvin, SD  57251
(605) 432-5528

**AMERICAN  INDIAN
HERITAGE FOUNDATION**
6051 Arlington Blvd.
Falls Church, VA  22044

**AMERICAN INDIAN
HISTORICAL SOCIETY**
1451 Masonic Ave.
San Francisco, CA  94117
(415) 626-5235

**AMERICAN INDIAN LORE ASSOC.**
P.O. Box 9698
Anaheim, CA 92802

**AMERICAN INDIAN RESEARCH
AND RESOURCE INSTITUTE**
Gettysburg College
P. O. Box 576
Gettysburg, PA  17325
(717) 337-6265

**AMERICAN  INDIAN SOCIETY**
P. O. Box 6431
Falls Church, VA  20002

**CENTER  FOR  PACIFIC
NORTHWEST STUDIES**
Western Washington University
High Street
Bellingham, WA  98225
(206) 676-3284/3125

**CHEROKEE HISTORICAL ASSOC.**
P.O. Box 398
Cherokee, NC 28719
(704) 497-2111

**CHEROKEE  NATIONAL
HISTORICAL  SOCIETY**
P.O. Box 515
Tahlequah, OK  74465
(918) 456-6007

CONFEDERATION OF AMERICAN
INDIANS
P.O. Box 5474
New York, NY 10163
(212) 972-1020

GATHERING OF NATIONS
P.O. Box 75102, Station 14
Alburquerque, NM 87194
(505) 836-2810

INSTITUTE OF EARLY AMERICAN
HISTORY AND CULTURE
P.O. Box 220
Williamsburg, VA 23187
(804) 253-5118

NATIONAL GEOGRAPHIC SOCIETY
17th & M Sts., N.W.
Washington, DC 20036
(202) 857-7000

NATIVE AMERICAN RESEARCH
INFORMATION CENTER
American Indian Institute
University of Oklahoma
Norman, OK 73069

NORTH AMERICAN INDIAN
WOMEN'S ASSOCIATION
P. O. Box 805
Eagle Butte, SD 57625

NORTHWEST INDIAN WOMEN'S
CIRCLE
P. O. Box 8279
Tacoma, WA 98408
(206) 458-7610

UNITED INDIANS OF ALL
TRIBES FOUNDATION
Day Break Star Arts Center
Discovery Park, Box C-99305
Seattle, WA 98199
(206) 285-4425